Mark Hopkins

The scriptural Idea of Man

Mark Hopkins

The scriptural Idea of Man

ISBN/EAN: 9783337062316

Printed in Europe, USA, Canada, Australia, Japan

Cover: Foto ©ninafisch / pixelio.de

More available books at **www.hansebooks.com**

THE

SCRIPTURAL IDEA OF MAN

Six Lectures

GIVEN BEFORE THE

THEOLOGICAL STUDENTS AT PRINCETON

ON

THE L. P. STONE FOUNDATION

BY

MARK HOPKINS D. D.

NEW YORK
CHARLES SCRIBNER'S SONS
1883

Copyright, 1883,
By CHARLES SCRIBNER'S SONS.

24298

PREFACE.

SOME eight years since I gave six lectures before the students in the Theological Seminary at New Haven. Those lectures were repeated at Chicago and at Oberlin, and portions of two of them were published in the "Princeton Review." As now published, they were delivered last March before the students of the Theological Seminary at Princeton. They have been modified, and to some extent rewritten, partly to meet changing phases of thought, and partly to avoid publishing again what had been already published, though portions of that have been retained when required by the connection. They are now published in accordance with the desire of the professors of the Seminary by whom I was invited to give them, and in the hope that they may be of service, not only to theological students, but to those, now increasing in number, who are interested in the subjects of which they treat.

M. H.

WILLIAMS COLLEGE, *June*, 1883.

CONTENTS.

LECTURE I.
MAN CREATED 1

LECTURE II.
MAN CREATED IN THE IMAGE OF GOD. — 1. IN KNOWLEDGE 24

LECTURE III.
IN KNOWLEDGE — *continued*. — 2. IN FEELING. — 3. IN FREEDOM. — 4. IN CAUSATIVE POWER 50

LECTURE IV.
THE MORAL NATURE 74

LECTURE V.
1. MAN CREATED WITH DOMINION. — 2. MAN, MALE AND FEMALE 98

LECTURE VI.
1. MAN IN HIS PRESENT STATE. — 2. THE MAN CHRIST JESUS 121

THE SCRIPTURAL IDEA OF MAN.

I.

MAN CREATED.

OF the first man the Scriptural idea is that he was created in the image of God. "So God created man in his own image, in the image of God created He him." This, if we connect with it the immediately following endowment of dominion over the earth, is the highest, the grandest, the most inspiring and ennobling idea and description of man ever given. There is in it essentially the idea of sonship, and so, of the fatherhood of God. In its fullness this was first revealed by Christ, but it was the Scriptural idea from the beginning. Without the image there is no sonship. With it, we have all that is implied in that, though the depth and fullness of the love of God as a Father could never have been apprehended except through Christ.

The image of God here spoken of is not the image of *a god*, such as man might form by personifying the objects or forces of nature, but of the God of the first chapter of Genesis, the One God, the Creator of the heavens and the earth and of man himself. Between the attributes of such a God and those of man the differences are as great as they can be, and leave the possibility that man should be in the image of God.

Here then we have, in the most ancient book known, an idea of God as One, and as the Creator. We have also an idea of man as immediately created by Him and in his image, that is not only consonant with the whole transcendent revelation of which it forms a part, but is at its basis. We have at the very beginning of the Old Testament a being worthy of the redemption revealed in the New Testament. Between man in the image of God, in personal relations with Him, spoken to, and intrusted with dominion over his world, and the provision made for his redemption when he had fallen and for his eternal life, there is a congruity essential to the unity of the Scriptures, and that could have been found in no other way.

Of man as thus in the image of God, the first thing that is asserted is, that he was created. "So God *created* man."

The word "create" may mean the absolute origination of material. This is its highest sense. It may also mean the formation, out of given materials, of something that did not exist before. This is a lower and secondary sense. That man was immediately formed out of material already existing the Bible asserts. Did that material always exist? or have we reason to believe that the very material out of which he was formed was previously originated, so that, if we trace it back, man was, in the fullest sense, created by God? If the material had an independent existence, it might, and probably would be, refractory, so that any one using it would be obliged to accommodate himself to the nature of the material; but if it was originated for a purpose, it would be adapted to that purpose, wholly flexible to the will of Him who originated it.

I know of no reason, *a priori*, why matter may not have existed always. I know of no law of interpretation that can make the word, "beginning," in the first verse of the Bible, more absolute than it is when Christ, speaking of marriage, says that "in the beginning it was not so." Nor do I know of any law of interpretation by which the word "created," in that verse, means an absolute origination more than it does when it is said that God created great whales, or created man.

But however this may be, with our present knowledge of matter it seems more rational to believe in its absolute origination. The argument is that from design, as in any other case. If we find in the qualities and quantities of the different kinds of matter, and also in their possible adaptation, evidences of design similar to those we find in the collocation and movements of matter, then we have the same kind of evidence that matter itself was originated, or, at least, did not always exist as matter, as we have that its collocations or movements were originated. And this evidence we do have in connection with every kind of matter. A single example will suffice. Oxygen is a kind of matter essential on this planet, but not necessarily existing everywhere. It has been said not to be in the sun, and if there at all, it is in a quantity relatively small. But look at the quantity here. There must have been, at first, just enough to combine chemically with the metallic bases, which, as oxides, constitute so large a part of the solid portion of the earth, and with hydrogen to constitute the water, and then to have just enough left free to mix with the nitrogen and form the atmosphere. This could not have been by chance, for in no medical prescription can exactness of quantity be more essential. Then look at its properties that fit it thus to combine and to form this mixture, and to be the vital element in the air and the supporter of combustion, and then, after having been the supporter of life, to be the agent in decomposing its structures and resolving them into their original elements. Of other substances, as of carbon, the adaptations are not less numerous. Again, if, instead of quality, we look at quantity alone, in its widest extent, as the kinds and systems of matter are related to each other, we shall be led to say that He "weighed the mountains in scales and the hills in a balance." We think it, therefore, more rational to suppose that these different kinds of matter were originated than that they existed from eternity, and with just such possible adaptations and quantities.

But you say it is inconceivable to you that a substantive being that did not exist before should be originated. Yes, but conceivability is not the limit of credibility. That is insisted on by Mill, in his Logic. It is not rational to suppose that we can conceive of any power or mode of its manifestation, unless we possess, in some degree, a similar power. The fact that such a power exists we may know; the mode of it we cannot know. A man wholly destitute of the organ of sight from the first, can neither conceive of what sight is nor of the mode of it. If, then, you know enough of the resources of an Infinite Being to know that He could not cause that to be which was not before, — to know that it would be either an absurdity or a contradiction, — then you must deny the fact of an original creation. But if you do not know so much, — and I am sure I do not, — then, aside from revelation, it seems to me that the hypothesis of the origination by mind, of what we call matter, in some way inconceivable to us, involves fewer difficulties than any other.

But whether created or not, the material being given, did man come to be man by the special act of Creator, or by evolution, or, which means the same thing, by development? This question, in view of recent speculations, we are bound to consider. In doing this, let us first understand our terms. In their strict meaning, *ev*olution implies something that had been *in*volved, and *de*velopment something that had been *en*veloped, in which each part of the now evolved or developed whole had a previous and separate existence. Such literal evolution as this is not claimed, but the doctrine of Professor Tyndall so approximates it that we shall understand ourselves if we call it a doctrine of evolution. That doctrine assumes the existence of the matter in the solar system in a nebulous state, and that there was in that matter "the promise and potency of all that now exists." Hence, his doctrine is, that the origin of man is from below, through the agency of forces inherent in matter, that these forces have been working upwards through vast periods, and that man is their highest product. Hence, "humanity" is the *grand etre* of Compte, and the only proper object of worship. Here the result is due to forces inherent in matter, and a system affirming this may be understood and accepted as a system of evolution. A result due to the superintending or contriving agency of a being that has an existence apart from the matter, and uses it, is not due to evolution, and can be said to be only by a use of the word that is misleading.

To a certain extent the language and statements of the Bible favor the doctrine of evolution as now stated. It is the *earth* that brings forth grass and herb and fruit tree; the *waters* that bring forth the moving creature that hath life, and the fowl that fly above the earth; and the earth again that brings forth cattle and creeping things. This is the language of evolution. But then we are told that God *commanded* the earth and the waters to do what they did, and we are also told expressly that He made everything that was made. Again, the Bible is in accord with evolution in revealing an upward movement, and through long periods. It is *not* in accord with it in saying that that movement was continuous; and it differs wholly from it in that we find at every point the agency and control of a personal God. All this is true of everything below man, but in the Bible account of *his* creation there is nothing that indicates any affinity with evolution. Then God did not call upon the earth or the waters, but simply said, "Let us make man."

Was man, then, created by God? or was he evolved from matter by forces inherent in that? That man was not thus evolved appears from the fact that, if he had been, the writer of the book of Genesis, the most ancient book known,[1] could not have had at that time, if at any time, ideas of God and of man congruous with what claims to be a revelation reaching on till the end of time, which has given to the nations accepting it the leadership in civilization, and which comprises a destiny for man the highest and grandest of which we can conceive. The conception of the unity of God, and so of Monotheism, in a system of worship, could not have been reached. How could it? The great argument for the unity of God, and the only argument within the reach of a being thus coming up from below, is from the unity of his works. But that unity was not then known. There was no science, and, looking at the diversity of nature both in her structures and tendencies, and at the seeming differences between the earth and the

---

[1] The current doctrine on this subject is assumed, but is not essential.

ocean and the heavens, we do not see how it would have been possible for man to reach the conception of the unity of the Author of nature, except through long processes of scientific observation. Equally difficult is it, if man came up from below, to see how the writer of the first chapter of Genesis could have had the idea of him as in the image of *such* a God. Those who hold that man did thus come up also hold that the first man was but slightly above the ape. They admit of no leap in the processes of nature At what point, then, or by what process, could the idea have come into the mind of the race, or of any one of them, that the first man was made in the image of the God who created the heavens and the earth, or that he had had directly deputed to him by that God, "dominion over the fish of the sea and the fowl of the air and over every living thing that moveth upon the earth?" That a being creeping up by insensible degrees from apehood, should ever have reached, and especially at that early period, the conception of himself as in the image of such a God, and as rightfully endowed with such a dominion, is impossible.

Again, place man thus coming up from an ape, or with any given powers, in the midst of an order of nature already established — and it must have been established when man appeared — and how could he have the conception of a primitive chaos out of which the order came? How of a being who could speak such a chaos into order by a word? It is only since the invention of the telescope and of the later discoveries in astronomy, geology, and chemistry, that science has come, or could come, to the idea of a primitive chaos. For me it is impossible to account for the idea of a primitive chaos in the mind of the writer of Genesis without revelation, and whether it would have occurred to scientific men even now, but for the Bible, may be doubted.[1]

In speaking further on this subject it may be observed, in a preliminary way, that evolution does not account for the origin of anything. It does not claim to, nor has it any advantage in the assumptions it must make. In assuming, as it does, the existence of nebulous matter, it puts itself on a level with those who assume the existence of a personal God. This, I say, because the whole difficulty lies in supposing the original and independent existence of anything. That *anything* should be, must forever remain a mystery, and the mystery that underlies one form of being is as great as that which underlies any other form of being. How being of any kind came to be, or that there should be being that never did come to be, we cannot comprehend. This is well expressed by Coleridge in his rhapsodical way: "Hast thou," says he, "ever raised thy mind to the consideration of EXISTENCE in and by itself as the mere act of existing? Hast thou ever said to thyself thoughtfully, IT IS! heedless in that moment whether it were a man before thee, or a flower, or a grain of sand? Without reference, in short, to this or that particular mode of existence? If thou hast indeed attained to this, thou wilt have felt the presence of a mystery

[1] See Appendix, Note A.

which must have fixed thy spirit in awe and wonder. The very words, There is nothing! or, There was a time when there was nothing! are self-contradictory. There is that within us which repels the proposition with as full and instantaneous a light, as if it bore evidence against the fact in the right of its own eternity. NOT TO BE, then is impossible. TO BE, incomprehensible."

That all men must thus know being is clear, but how far they all consider it thoughtfully, and attain to the wonder spoken of by Coleridge, is not so clear. To the brute, and also to many persons, the mere fact of being is a matter of course. If they are surprised, or wonder, it is not that anything is, but that something is different from what it has been accustomed to be. To be surprised at what is new has its use in the mechanism of a being related to time. It puts it on the alert to guard against possible dangers in new combinations, but a capacity to wonder at BEING, of necessity coeval with a past that had no beginning, can have no relation to the wants of time. Such wonder could not be in a being evolved from an ape. It must belong to one capable of apprehending infinity, and who, if not related to that duration which has had no beginning, is yet ready to be swept on in the current of that which has no end.

Of this philosophical wonder it should be observed, because it bears on our ground of belief, that its tendency is not, like that of ordinary wonder, to diminish through familiarity, but rather the reverse. Awakened by the fact of being, necessarily involving the idea of being uncreated; also by the discovery of the immensity, and order, and movements, and adaptations of that around us which we call the cosmos, it increases as its object is dwelt upon till it becomes utter bewilderment. Whoever, therefore, recognizes all this, and accepts it as a reality, ought to have no difficulty on account of its strangeness merely, in accepting any form of the manifestation of being that may claim his acceptance. That there should, for instance, be a future life under a different form cannot be more strange than that there should be the present life under its present form. That there should be a heaven hereafter cannot be more strange than that there should be a happy family here. That there should be spiritual existence cannot be stranger than is material existence. That there should be a personal God, infinite and holy, cannot be more strange than that we should be personal beings, as we are, and that there should be this multiform universe in which we find ourselves. Indeed, I think we may say, that live as long as we may during the eternal ages, go where we may into the depths of infinite space, we shall never find a scene of things more strange and wonderful than we are in now.

Plainly, then, if we go back to the origin of things the evolutionist has no advantage over others. We have, at least, as much ground for assuming the existence of a personal God as he has for assuming that of nebulous matter. There is not a single difficulty that stands in the way of one assumption that does not stand in the way of the other, while the difficulties that follow from the assumption of matter are immeasurably greater than those that follow from the assumption of a personal God. In one case the primary assumption solves everything, in the other it not only solves nothing, but requires constantly either new assumptions of origin, or a violation of the law of causality.

This will be seen if we concede to the evolutionist his nebulous matter as having had an independent existence. We then ask, Whence came life? Was it inherent? Did it remain diffused through the matter during those vast sweltering periods while the mass was cooling, or was it newly originated? Then, giving him life thus diffused, or newly originated, whence the organism? Or, giving him what Professor Tyndall assumes, "A low organism vaguely sensitive all over," whence the necessary environment, the light, the warmth, the food? Whence the organs by which these are appropriated? These, we are told, are differentiated. But by what? We are told again, by differentiation.* The organs, as the stomach and liver, the eye and the ear, are differentiated by differentiation!—which is, of course, satisfactory. Or, if any one would know more particularly how the eye was formed originally, let him read the account of it by Professor Tyndal, in which he says, the formation was begun by the rays of light falling upon "pigment cells," in an organization vaguely sensitive all over! But again, given such an organism, how could it be propagated? Whence the sexual relation, so universal in its presence, and so diversified in its forms? How, through so wide a range of vegetables and animals, could two individuals of opposite sexes be evolved through those long ages so as to come to perfection at the same time? How could the individuals have been preserved until that time? Or, if we suppose all the above to be given, whence that upward tendency to which both geology and the Scriptures testify? That tendency involves a law, not of evolution, but of upbuilding. It involves a law of the forces and products of this universe that enters into its whole construction. It is the law of the conditioning and conditioned, in accordance with which the universe is built up by a constant increase as we go up of the number of forces at work, and a constant diminution of the sphere within which they work. Of course, at each upward step we must have a new force, and one so far superior to all below as to be able to control them. Such higher force is, indeed, revealed only as it controls the lower. It comes by addition, and can be supposed to have come from below only by supposing that a higher and controlling force can come out of one that is lower and controlled. This necessitates a process of upbuilding from without in which that which is below is a condition, but not a cause of that which is above. Such a law would secure the upward tendency, but could not produce evolution or be produced by it.

There is, I know, an attempt made to account for the upward tendency by what is called the law of the survival of the fittest. This does not account for it, for, first, it does not apply to that upward movement by which lower forms of life and inferior races are succeeded in the order of time by higher forms, and superior races. According to geology, as well as the Scriptures, the lower orders of animals are the most ancient, and man, the highest of all, has been introduced at a comparatively recent date. Man did not survive; he came. And if he came as man, naked, weaponless, relatively feeble, with the prolonged helplessness of infancy, he was of all creatures least fitted to survive. With no experience and no determinate instinct, such as avails the animal for self-preservation, it is difficult to see how he could have survived. No law of the survival of the fittest could, therefore, have had anything to do with his coming and place. He came latest, because those conditions of the earth and of the animals that were needed by him were latest reached. We see, therefore, that the law of the survival of the fittest has no relation to the greatest and most important part of the upward movement. Nor, except by an equivocal use of the word "fittest," can this law account for any upward movement among contemporaneous plants and animals. It is simply the law of the survival of the strongest with no reference to the usefulness or value of that which survives. It is the tautological proposition of the survival of that which is fittest to survive. Sow wheat and Canada thistles together, and let them fight their own battle, and which will survive? Over the larger portion of the earth, if not the whole of it, leave those grains and fruits that nourish man to an unaided struggle and they will be destroyed. The weeds, the thorns, the thistles, are fittest to survive, and it is by this very law that the sentence originally pronounced on man, " In the sweat of thy brow shalt thou eat thy bread," is carried into execution. It is only by the sweat of the brow that the survival of that which is *fittest for man* is secured. So too with animals. The stronger and more fierce, the lions, and tigers, and wolves, are fittest to survive, and nothing but a law which no evolution can account for, that the weaker animals shall be more prolific, can secure the survival of those weaker and fittest for the service of man. Nothing, then, but the agency of man, and a law of fertility that could have originated only from a comprehensive prevision, has caused the survival of the plants and animals that are fittest for the use of man. Evolution cannot account for the tendency and movement upward, and makes no provision for it.

It is generally supposed that the doctrine of Darwin, on the origin of species, gives support to the theory of evolution. It tends in that direction, and may do it on two conditions. The first is, that there be produced at least one well-established instance of the origin of one species from another. That has not been done. Varieties within a species, as of pigeons, there are without limit; but there is no instance of the change of a pigeon into an eagle, or of any tendency in that direction. The second condition is, that it shall be shown that, if such a change were possible, it must be from lower to higher. This cannot be shown. Species often degenerate.

On the whole, then, I think we may now say that evolution, in the form in which we have now spoken of it, is not only atheistic, for it is that of course, but that it does not account for the origin of man.

But is the evolution above spoken of that which is now commonly known as evolution? Is it that of Mr. Herbert Spencer?

Mr. Spencer speaks of a power unknown and unknowable, by which the results ascribed to evolution are brought about. Does he, or does he not, say that this power is inherent in matter so as to be one of its constituents? If he does say that, he is properly an evolutionist. If he does not say it, but says that the results are due to the action of a being, knowable or unknowable, that is separate from matter and uses it, then he is not properly an evolutionist.[1] That there has been, through long periods, a process of change from simpler to more complex forms, or, in the language of Mr. Spencer, from homogeneity to heterogeneity, the Bible asserts. To account for this, we may either say that there has been what I have called evolution, or the agency of a personal God; and in either case we understand ourselves and can use words with a definite meaning. But if we introduce between these a power that is claimed to be distinct from matter, and yet is unknown and unknowable, it is easy to see what complications and misleading use of terms will be sure to follow. The way is, then, open for each person to know as much or as little of this unknowable being as may be conveni-

[1] See Appendix, Note B.

ent in any discussion, and for as great differences between evolutionists as there are among theologians.

That Mr. Spencer does not only admit but affirm the existence of a power distinct from matter and that uses it, I suppose is true. It certainly is if we accept as a fair exposition of his system the elaborate and careful account of it by Professor Fiske at the dinner given in New York, last winter, in honor of Mr. Spencer. Professor Fiske is among the ablest disciples of Mr. Spencer in this country, and I suppose his speech may be fairly taken as representing the system. In that system we have the prevalent form of what calls itself evolution. This, it was claimed in New York, is already established and triumphant, and as the account given by it of the origin of man differs so essentially from that of the Bible, we may not pass it without notice.

Professor Fiske is distinct and full in his affirmation of the existence of an unknowable power distinct from matter. The power is said to be unknowable, but he knows it to *be*. So much he knows and affirms, though how he knows it, except as we know the being of a personal God, does not appear. He says further, quoting Matthew Arnold, that this power is "a power, not ourselves, that makes for righteousness." He knows, further, that to this power "no limit in time or space is conceivable," and that "all the phenomena of the universe, whether they be what we call material, or what we call spiritual phenomena, are manifestations of the infinite and eternal Power." He further knows that this eternal

Power that thus manifests itself in every event of the universe, "is, in the deepest possible sense, the author of the moral law." He also speaks, in connection with this power, of "a *divine* sanction for holiness" and a "divine condemnation of sin." He further knows that this infinite and eternal being is capable of an effort, and an enormous effort, through untold ages. He says, "When you say of a moral belief or a moral sentiment, that it is a product of evolution, you imply that it is something which the universe, through untold ages, has been laboring to bring forth, and you ascribe to it a value proportionate to the enormous effort that it has cost to produce it." Here we have the *whole universe*, the infinite and eternal being included, laboring, "through untold ages," to bring forth a *moral sentiment*, and bringing it forth with ENORMOUS effort! Of course there was in the universe, during those long ages, no moral sentiment. The infinite and eternal being did not have any, and we may well inquire whether it knew what was coming, and what it thought of it when it did come. The truth is, that, on this theory, a moral sentiment was a creation. The evolutionist may say what he will about its having lain, during these untold ages, enveloped in the universe, it was really a thing absolutely new, and unless there were a previous being who knew what moral sentiment is, its appearance in man can be accounted for in accordance with no law of causation that we know anything about.

And as evolutionists of this class thus know some things about what this unknowable being is and does, so also do they know some things that it is not and does not do. These things it did not come in the way of Professor Fiske to state, but it is well understood that evolutionists know that this being is not a person. They never apply to it the personal pronouns. Of course they know that it has no self-consciousness. They also know that this being does not contrive. Evolutionists scout the idea that those numberless and marvelous adaptations and adjustments which men generally have attributed to a contriving mind are any evidence of contrivance at all.

So much evolutionists of this class know of what this unknowable being is and does: and so much they know of what it is not and does not do; and this knowledge they do not have as "dogmas handed down by priestly tradition, but as *scientific* knowledge." I have thus stated it that you may know what this system is which gives us an account of the origin of man so different from that of the Bible, and also to call your attention to two things. The first, already alluded to, is the indefinite and misleading use of terms that must follow the introduction of such an unknowable, intermediate, indefinite element into our discussions. In connection with such a being and with such a genesis of moral sentiments, what place have we for such terms as sin and holiness, moral law and *divine* sanctions? And yet they are used as the livery of heaven to clothe evolution in, while such words as redemption, repentance, forgiveness, salvation, are wholly unknown.

The second thing to which I call your attention is

the attempt of Professor Fiske and others to reconcile what they call science with religion. And by science here is meant this form of evolution, for we are expressly told that the knowledge that the unknowable being is, and the knowledge of what it does, is science. This reconciliation Professor Fiske thinks he has accomplished to such an extent that "that phantom of the hostility between religion and science which has been the abiding terror of timid and superficial minds, is exorcised now and forever." What, then, does this reconciliation amount to? To a reconciliation with Christianity? Certainly not. Christianity affirms that God can be known, and that to know the only true God, and Jesus Christ, whom He hath sent, is eternal life. This science, if we must call it so, says of the infinite and eternal power, that *it* is unknown and unknowable; and it was hardly ingenuous in Professor Fiske to say that Mr. Spencer meant by his unknowableness pretty much what the Scriptures mean when they say of God that we are unable "to find Him out." Christianity says,— precious and glorious truth,— that God is a Father, and clothes Him with the attributes of a Father. This science says that its power is not a person, and denies to it every attribute of a father. Christianity comes to us as a direct revelation from God, and as confirmed by miracles. Evolution says that such revelation is impossible, and a miracle preposterous. It knows scientifically that the Infinite and Eternal Power could not make a revelation or work a miracle. Christianity says that God hears prayer. Evolution denies it, and pities those who believe it. They lack scientific insight. Christianity says that God is to be worshipped in spirit and in truth. Evolution denies that. An impersonal being cannot be worshipped. Christianity says that God is to be loved. Evolution wholly rules out this highest and transscendent expression of our spirits in their relation to God. It says that the Infinite and Eternal Power does not love us, and is not an object of love. Evidently, then, Evolution can be reconciled with Christianity only by destroying it. Can it, then, be reconciled with any other religion? No. No system that denies a personal God can have an object of worship, or be rationally made the basis of a religion. If this is the way the phantom is to be exorcised, I fear that "timid and superficial minds" will be haunted for some time to come.

Having thus spoken of the prevalent objections to the Scriptural statement of the origin of man, we now pass to that.

That statement is, that man, so far as he is physical, was *created* out of matter previously existing. Around this statement peculiar mystery is supposed to gather. But does it?[1] Possibly our difficulty in regard to the act or process of creation may arise in part or wholly from our not perceiving that there is really equal mystery connected with that to which we are accustomed, and to which custom alone blinds us. Here is a man of full stature and perfect in form. Twenty-six years ago he did not exist. The materials of which his body is composed existed, but they

[1] See Appendix, Note C.

were as wide asunder as the poles. The lime was in the earth, the water in the ocean, the carbon and the nitrogen were floating in the air, perhaps over the Rocky Mountains or the Himalayas. By some process or power these materials have been brought together and fashioned into bones and muscles and the organs of the senses, and here the man is. *And nobody wonders at it!* It is a matter of course. The evolutionist, making no distinction between evolution and growth, so radically different, says the man has been evolved. Evolved! when not one particle of matter or a lineament of form now in him was in the cell from which his growth began; when, in fact, there was no cell! Evolved! No, he grew, and by a power and process of which philosophers and scientists know as little as Topsy did when she said, "I 'spect I growed;" as little as they do of the power and process by which the same materials might have been brought together in an act or process of creation. Keeping in mind the distinction already made between common and philosophic wonder, the bringing together of these materials in a moment, and giving them life by an original act or process that might be called creation, would be no more strange than the bringing of them together in twenty-six years by an act and process of growth. We know as much of one as we do of the other.

I have taken man as an instance. He is of slow growth, and perhaps the illusion connected with time would be less if we were to look first at an acre of land perfectly bare on the first day of April, and then again on the first day of July, when it is covered with *four tons* of organized matter in the shape of clover, every stalk and leaf and blossom perfect. Where were those four tons of matter on the first day of April? And what do you know of the process by which it has been brought together and fashioned into its forms, when you pronounce the word *growth?*

Life and organization we know did not always exist on this planet. There must, therefore, have been a beginning to both. No matter how far you go back, only do not get bewildered in the mists of those long periods. Time has nothing to do with causation. There must have been a beginning, and that beginning could not have been after the mode of generation and growth which we now see. It must have been a creation. It may have been by an act or a process. The method is wholly unknown to us, but if we had been accustomed to see bodies originated by an immediate creation it would have been no more surprising to us than it now is to see them originated by the method of growth. Admitting this, as I think we must, we gain nothing, philosophically or in any way, by limiting the range of the creative energy and method. We need, therefore, find no difficulty in accepting the statement of the Bible, "So God *created* man."

II.

MAN IN THE IMAGE OF GOD. — IN KNOWLEDGE.

The Scriptural proposition, that God created man, we have considered. We now proceed to consider the further proposition, that He created him in his own image.

In what did this image consist? If we would get the Scriptural idea we must go to the record. Doing this, we observe, in the first place, the prominence and significance given to the creation of man by the form of the narrative. Everything below him had been finished and pronounced good, but now the work was to be completed. The great work, the crowning work, the light upon the top of the lighthouse, that towards which all the rest had looked forward and converged, was now to be done, and nothing could better indicate the greatness of this work than the arrest in the progress of the narrative, and the grandeur of the characteristic to be given to it. What had before been done manifested the attributes of God unconsciously, but now there was to be a being in his very image, capable of gathering up and consciously expressing the inarticulate praise of all that was below him.

Looking further at the narrative, the plain impression from it is, that the image of God to be thus created was not anything incidental, or that could be separated from man, but must consist in something so essential to him that if he should lose it he would cease to be man. "And God said, Let us create man in our image," the idea of the image evidently entering in as an element in the conception of the creative act, so that when the creative act was completed, and before Adam had acted in any way, he was in the image of God. If not, it cannot be said that God created man in his image. If we suppose, as we must, that there was a time when God completed *his* work, and gave the man over to his own control, it must follow, if God created him in his image, that that image was completed at that moment, and as it had not existed previously in anything that had been created, it must have consisted in the essential difference or differences between man and the creatures below him. These differences are found mainly, first, in the intellect of man regarded as rational; second, in his moral and spiritual nature; and third, in his freedom, including the great fact that man is, and the brute is not, a proper and responsible cause. God is a proper cause, and if man were not, he could not be in his image. So long, therefore, as man continues to be rational, moral, and free, and hence capable of knowing God, he will be in his image; and when he ceases to be rational, moral, and free, he will be no longer man.

This point needs attention, because it has been supposed by some that the image of God here spoken of consisted in knowledge and moral character, or holiness, rather than in the substantive being, or in the powers with which man was endowed. By the fall man lost the moral character by which he was in the image of God, but the Scriptures do not give us the impression that he lost that image of God in which he was created. This appears, because the presence of that image, as still remaining, is assumed in the reason given in Genesis for the death penalty: "He that sheddeth man's blood by man shall his blood be shed, for in the image of God created He him." It is implied also in that wonderful and endearing appellation by which our Saviour has taught us to draw nigh to God, saying, "Our Father." This term I suppose He intended to authorize all men to use, and that in the use of it, with the full understanding of its import, there is implied that image of God in which he was created. It is in this image of God, too, that we find the ground of that love of God to the race which expressed itself in giving his Son to die for it. It is the fact that man has dignity and value, as in the image of God, that accounts for and justifies that great transaction. Not towards a being that was in his image as holy was his love shown, for "God commendeth his love towards us in that, while we were yet sinners, Christ died for us," but towards a being whom He still permits to call him Father, on the ground of that image in which He created him. In this image it is that we find the ground of our respect for the race, and for our appeal to men to forsake what is low and base, and to enter upon a pilgrimage that shall bring them to their Father's house.

But however this may be, if man was made in the image of God in knowledge, he must have been made in his image in the powers through which the knowledge came to be. What powers of knowledge, then, and what kinds of knowledge, has man? Here we have the powers and their products, but as we know the powers only through the products we will speak of these first.

Of the infant mind in what must have been its nebulous condition we know, and can know, but little; but the first thing that must be assumed and affirmed by one who would carry on an intelligent intellectual process must be his own existence. This he must affirm and be sure of before he can have the right to affirm anything else. The claim to be an absolute agnostic is an absurdity. It involves intellectual suicide. As I have said elsewhere, if a man is to have the right to begin at all he must begin with certainty. For if he were to say, I am not certain that I exist, I doubt it, he might be asked, Are you certain that you doubt? If he were to say, Yes, that would be to begin with certainty. If he were to say No, we should ask him what right he has to be troubling people with his doubts before he is certain he has them. We should certainly require him either to keep on doubting till he should be certain of his doubts, or to hold his peace. Except on the assumption and implied assertion that a man exists he cannot think, or feel, or act. He cannot say, *I.*

It is so involved in all that he does that he can have no right to do anything without it. We are thus compelled to assume that we exist. It is not a matter of choice or of will. If we claim to doubt or deny it, the doubt or denial assumes it. We thus have the test of necessity, which I hold to be the only adequate test.

Having thus by necessity, and with no intervention of the will, a knowledge that we exist, what else do we know in the same way; or if not in the same way, with equal certainty? We know with equal certainty all those things in regard to which a distinction can be made between the order of time and the order of nature, and which are first in the order of nature. Thus, in knowing our own existence we know first in the order of time our thought, or some affection of the mind, and then we know that in the order of nature our existence must have been before our thought. The thought we know directly, existence, or ourselves as existing, we know in knowing the thought. There is no inference. Both are known in one concrete act. It is thus that we know space in knowing body, time in knowing succession, and cause in knowing events. With the ideas thus given there are truths immediately connected; as, that every body must be in space, and every event must, not may, but *must*, have a cause. These we believe by necessity. We are so constituted that we must believe them.

These ideas and truths are a class by themselves. The ideas are given and the truths affirmed by what is called the reason, and are essentially different from single truths immediately known by sense or intuition. By Reid they were called principles of common sense, and by Dugald Stewart fundamental laws of human belief. By some they have been called transcendental ideas and truths, and there is in them all there is that is solid in the nebulous transcendentalism that has been in our sky for the last fifty years. These ideas and truths are involved in our several mental processes as mathematical axioms, and mere intuitions are not. Hence they are a different logical element, are of much greater importance, and should be ranked as first truths.

The truths of this class, and the same may be said of mathematical axioms, are first seen in some particular instance, but pass at once into a general form. They do so by a process of what may be called extension, but it is so elementary that it has not received a name. Naturally, and almost universally, the terms generalization, and induction, have been applied to processes in which these ideas and truths are involved, but they are misleading. The logical principle is not the same. In generalization and induction the underlying principle is resemblance, and through them absolute certainty cannot be reached. But here the underlying principle is identity, and we are as certain of the general, as of the particular truth. As soon as we understand the terms we know at once, with no repetition of instances, that every body must be in space as certainly as we know that one body is in space. And so of causation. We are as certain that every event must have a cause as we are that one event has a cause. By applying generalization and induction in this connection we either give to those processes a validity that does not belong to them, or cast suspicion upon a process that gives certainty.

Of the truths now mentioned the test, as I have said, is necessity. Not only do all men believe them, but they must. Here is a truth which man is forced to believe by the constitution of his mind. No passion, or bias, or influence of will can intervene; and if we may not rely on a result thus reached, our faculties are not reliable, and we are landed in universal skepticism. This test of necessity is decisive of itself, but it involves, of course, self-evidence and universality, while they do not involve it. What is necessarily believed must be universally believed, and must have self-evidence. That universality of belief is a sufficient test of truth no one claims. It was once universally believed that the heavenly bodies move round the earth. The difficulty with self-evidence as a sufficient test is, not only that it does not include the others, but especially that we have no test of a self-evident truth. What is self-evident to one man may not be so to another. It is said that the larger part of the propositions in the first book of Euclid were self-evident to Sir Isaac Newton. They are not so to most men. To Dr. McCosh, as stated in his Criteria, it seems self-evident that two straight lines cannot enclose a space. John S. Mill says in his logic, that "it is an induction from the evidence of our senses." We have also for the class of truths now in question two tests which do not apply except to them as necessary, and which enable us to deal effectually with perverse and uncandid men. One is, that though a man may deny one of these truths in words he is compelled to act as though he believed it. He cannot deny his own existence, or that a body must be in space, and move at all, without acting as if he believed those truths. The other test is, that, deny them as vehemently as he may, we have yet a right to treat him as though he believed them. If a man who is sentenced to receive thirty-nine lashes well laid on would escape by affirming that he does not exist, we might comfort him with the assurance that in that case it would not hurt him, but we should still lay them on. In no other case is it allowable to impute to men opinions or beliefs which they disavow. To many men it may appear self-evident that deceit is always wrong, yet if a man were to say that it does not appear so to him he would neither be compelled to act as if it did so appear, nor should we have a right to treat him as if it did.[1]

Here then we have a class of truths fully authenti-

---

[1] On this point of necessity as a test of truth, as also on the use of generalization and induction in connection with these truths, I am compelled to differ from Dr. McCosh in his *Criteria of Diverse Truths*, recently published. He there objects to necessity as a test, because it "sounds too much like fatality to be agreeable to the free spirit of man." It may not be agreeable to the free spirit of man to be under the necessity of existing; but if he must be, as he is, under that necessity, I see no objection to his being under the necessity of believing that he exists.

cated. Between them and truths simply intuitive or self-evident, the line is distinct. When the question is brought before a man whether two straight lines can inclose a space, it may be self-evident that they cannot. He may even be necessitated to believe it, as I think a man always is necessitated to believe an intuitive truth, but he may live a lifetime without having the question brought before him. Not so with any one of the truths of reason. He cannot live at all without knowing his own being, his personal identity, and his causative power, and so of others. Intuitive or self-evident truths he *may* know; the truths of reason he *must* know.

Man then, knowing himself to be, and having these truths thus authenticated and incorporated into his very being, is able to turn his gaze inward upon himself, to know himself as distinct from all other beings, and to say *I.* This is a great thing, — this finding of himself. It is what no being below man can do. Thus doing, he finds among the ideas and truths thus given all those by which he is constituted a person, and made in the image of God.

Of discussions concerning the ideas and truths now spoken of, three things are to be said. The first is, that if those ideas and truths are what they claim to be, mankind do not really differ concerning them. All men must not only have the ideas and believe the truths, but they must be essentially, in their relations and processes, the same to all. The second is, that the more intimately these ideas and truths are wrought into our very being, the more difficult they are of correct apprehension and statement. The third thing is, that when they are once clearly stated they seem the simplest and plainest of all truths, and what every man has known all his life. From this it will follow that we have encouragement to endeavor to bring these ideas and truths into full light; and, also, that in doing so, the difficulty must be largely in an ambiguous and unsteady use of terms. Having myself been perplexed by the use made of terms in this department, quite as much, perhaps, as by the subject itself, I doubt if I can serve you better than by turning aside for a little to call your attention to it in some particulars. "Words are things." They are not only the product, but the instrument of thought, and these act and react on each other. It is, therefore, of prime importance that you should have, both in your thinking and speaking, precision and uniformity in the use of these terms, which must be involved in all your speculations as ministers, and enter largely into the staple of your discourses.

Instead of being a form of knowledge, the truths I have spoken of are represented as being something different from it. They are said to underlie it. In speaking of this I must refer to Dr. Calderwood. In doing so, and in differing from him on certain points, I wish to express my high appreciation of him in every respect, and especially of the courtesies shown me by him. "All knowledge," says Dr. Calderwood, "rests on faith."[1] In illustrating this he says: "In the very exercise of its powers of knowledge the

---

[1] *Philosophy of the Infinite*, chap. iii.

mind rests on the belief that our senses and consciousness are trustworthy, and not deceptive witnesses. In contemplating and comparing objects all knowledge is accepted and arranged on the conviction that a thing cannot be, and not be, at the same time. Through all the varieties of thought, feeling, and volition, we believe in our own identity."

In this passage we have the four words to which I call your attention: knowledge, belief, faith, and consciousness. And first, of the first three. In the passage quoted we have faith identified with belief, as is constantly done by Hamilton, Mansel, and others of that school. They identify faith with belief, and then knowledge is made to rest upon it. But to one using terms in their ordinary sense what can be more confusing than this? By all ordinary usage knowledge is a stronger word than belief, and yet the stronger is made to rest on the weaker. I *know* what happened yesterday; I yet do not know that I am the same person to-day that I was yesterday. I know there is such a city as New York, and yet I do not know that it is impossible for a thing to be and not to be at the same time. That I only believe. Again, it is said by Dr. Calderwood that "The province of faith is much more extensive than that of knowledge." "Belief," he goes on, "affords a foundation for knowledge, and at the same time stretches far beyond it." In its ordinary sense belief does indeed stretch far beyond knowledge, but only as it gathers a shade of uncertainty, whereas, as used by Dr. Calderwood, belief can stretch far beyond knowledge only as it is more certain. With this view of Dr. Calderwood many philosophers coincide. Sir William Hamilton says: "In the order of nature belief always precedes knowledge." Professor Christlieb says: "All knowledge is in the last instance conditioned by faith, and faith (that is, an act of belief) is the preliminary and the medium of every act of intelligence."[1] To illustrate this he says: "It is by the direct testimony of our own minds that we are convinced of the fact that we exist, think, walk, and dream; and this fact neither needs nor is capable of proof. We merely *believe it*. The certainty of our thinking depends simply on an act of belief." He goes further and becomes mystical. "Faith," he says, "from the invisible world in which it lives, must bring the truths unattainable by Reason and impart them to her."[2]

Now, it seems to me that in all this these great men have greatly perplexed a simple subject. For what is it? I agree with President Porter, that to know is to be certain of something. I stick a stake there. I insist upon it that we must have certainty to begin with, or we can never have a right to begin. If therefore to know is to be certain, then whatever gives us certainty gives us knowledge, and nothing else does. We know only so far as we are certain. So far as we are certain we know. That there are different modes of attaining certainty I agree. We may be certain of our personal identity, or that a thing cannot be and not be at the same time, by the

[1] *Modern Doubt and Christian Belief*, p. 124.
[2] Ibid., p. 127.

necessary action of our faculties. Than this no certainty can be greater, and if we do not know these, what, I ask, do we know? There may also be certainty through the senses, and through the operation of the understanding; but however it may come, I hold that certainty reached by a rational being in any way constitutes knowledge, and that any faith, or belief, or conviction, short of certainty, is not knowledge. In the operations of the intellect I admit of no mysticism. The results of those operations, whether necessary, or under the control of the will, I divide into two classes. Of some I am certain, and in that certainty is knowledge. Of others I am not certain, and then I have belief, or opinion, with its varying shades. If I am certain, I am bound as a rational being to know the ground of that certainty, and I may not rest and say I am certain till the ground is sufficient. If I hold an opinion or belief, I am bound to know the ground of the opinion or belief. That is the whole of it. I admit of no province of faith in the sense in which Dr. Calderwood uses that word, that is, as he says, much more extensive, or any more extensive than that of knowledge. I admit of no faith "that lives in the invisible world and brings truths unattainable by Reason, and imparts them to her." If truths are to be brought from the invisible world it must be by some being, and not by faith, and must be received, if received at all, on the ground of adequate evidence. Faith, — belief of any kind regarded as mere belief, except as based on evidence, — what is it but weakness and folly?

I regard it as specially unfortunate that *faith*, a term so central and vital in our religion, should be used in senses so different from that in which it is used in the Scriptures. And this is the more disastrous, because the term seems, often at least, to be used in this way with an entire unconsciousness that there is any difference. Thus Sir William Hamilton, after saying that faith is the organ by which we apprehend what is beyond our knowledge, adds: "In this all divines and philosophers worthy of the name are found to coincide."[1] In his chapter on the province of faith and of reason, Dr. Calderwood says: "It is necessary to premise that in treating at present of the province of faith, I refer exclusively to that exercise of faith which is found in the consciousness of our primary or fundamental beliefs." "Such beliefs," he adds, "if they have any value at all, are nothing less than the foundation and guarantee of all our thoughts. " Here Dr. Calderwood identifies faith with beliefs, and makes it consist of those primary beliefs that are given by what Hamilton calls the Regulative Faculty. True he says: "Faith may also find exercise in connection with the facts of experience, or with inferences drawn from these." But this is not true of faith except as the meaning of the word is changed, and of that he gives no intimation. The faith that finds exercise in connection with the facts of experience is wholly a different thing under the same name, and neither is at all the faith of the Bible. How wholly the faith now spoken of differs

---

[1] *Metaphysics*, p. 531.

from that of the Bible will be readily seen if we compare the two. The one is involuntary and necessary; the other voluntary and may be commanded. "Have faith in God." One admits of no degrees; the other does. "Lord, increase our faith." One belongs to all men; the other does not. "All men have not faith." One implies no previous belief; the other does. In the one there is no element of confidence in a person; in the other there is, and the faith cannot be rational unless the confidence be well founded. The faith of the Bible always rests on a person as its object or ground, and has in it a voluntary element. It manifests itself in belief, in obedience, and in commitment; in believing what a person says because he says it — in doing what he commands because he commands it, and in committing to him without reserve all that he offers himself to us for. Abraham believed God, and it was counted to him for righteousness. That was faith. When commanded to go out from his own country, not knowing whither he went, he obeyed. That was faith. And when Paul committed his soul to Christ, knowing whom he believed, and that He was able to keep it against that day, that was faith. Here we have constantly trust in a person and the voluntary element. How different all this is from any primitive and necessary belief that is part of our nature I need not say. The two are, indeed, in different spheres. They involve logical elements wholly different, and that they should be treated of under the same name, and be so far identified as they constantly are, — wholly so, as it seems to me, by Sir

William Hamilton, — is an evil that ought, if possible, to be remedied.

We thus see that the faith of the Bible is a principle wholly rational and practical. It is no nondescript "organ," by which we apprehend what is beyond our knowledge. Nor is it a principle by which we apprehend the invisible. There are those, as Dr. Christlieb, who say that we have a principle by which we apprehend the invisible, and call that faith. But if we apprehend the invisible at all, as we do — certainly we apprehend invisible magnetism — we apprehend it as we do anything else, either directly, or by inference, and we do it with the ordinary powers of apprehension which God has given us. We need for this no new organ or principle called faith. No mere power of apprehension, call it what you may, has, or can have, any moral character; nor can it be properly identified or even classed with the faith required in the Bible.

Knowledge, belief, faith, — these we have considered, and now pass to the third word mentioned, consciousness. As this has been used, and is now, it has, perhaps, been productive of more confusion than either of the others.

According to Sir William Hamilton, consciousness cannot be defined. "It is," he says, "the general form of all our mental operations, and so there is no higher genus under which it can be brought."[1] "It is," he says, "an actual and not a potential knowledge; an immediate and not a mediate knowledge."

[1] *Metaphysics*, lect. xi.

He says, also, — which looks much like a definition, — that "the most general characteristic of consciousness is the recognition by the thinking subject of its own acts or affections."[1] Also, that consciousness gives us not only a knowledge of the acts and affections of the thinking subject, but also of its existence and individuality, and continuous identity. Also, that it testifies to the existence of an external world, inasmuch as we know that there is an external world, and if we are conscious of the knowledge, we must be also of the thing known. The authority of consciousness, as thus defined or described, he says cannot be denied unless we deny the possibility of philosophy, because "philosophy is only a scientific development of the facts which consciousness reveals."[1] He says, of course, that consciousness is not a separate faculty dependent for its action on the will, but always acts in connection with the action of each faculty. If the intellect acts in the way of knowing, then consciousness acts in knowing that we know. If the sensibility acts in the way of feeling, then consciousness acts by necessity in knowing that we feel. With these statements President Porter agrees in general, but he says there is a primary and a secondary consciousness, the first possessed by all men, the second attained only by a few. This division he makes on the ground of increased attention, and he may well make it if, with Hamilton, he makes attention a form of consciousness. Primary consciousness, he defines with Hamilton as

[1] *Metaphysics*, lect. xi.

"the power which the mind naturally and necessarily possesses of knowing its own acts and states." Dr. Mansel says, "It is by consciousness alone that we know that God exists, or that we are able to offer Him any service."[1] He also speaks of the religious consciousness, and tells how it is built up. In his "Philosophy of the Infinite," speaking of the capacity of man to know that God is and also what He is, Dr. Calderwood, the successor of Sir William Hamilton, says, "In this, as in every other philosophical question, the inquiry is restricted exclusively to an examination of consciousness." Again, "The method of inquiry is nothing more than a careful interpretation of consciousness." "This method," he continues, "Sir William Hamilton has not followed, and therefore his theory is, as it seems to me, in many of its parts a misrepresentation of consciousness."

Here we have a word as elastic as the tent in the Arabian Nights, that could serve for a single man and be carried in his pocket, or be stretched over an army. Now consciousness is the general form of all our mental operations, and now it is the actual and immediate knowledge by the mind of its own acts and affections. Now, again, it is a knowledge, — and they all agree in this, — not of the acts and affections of the mind, but of its existence and individuality and continued identity, a form of knowledge that lies wholly in a different sphere. Now it is a knowledge not only of the states of the mind, but also of the ex-

[1] *Limits of Religious Thought*, p. 64.

ternal world. Now it simply takes cognizance of a single mental fact, and now it is that on which depends our knowledge of God. Now this knowledge is immediate and direct and authoritative, and now it needs to be interpreted, and this interpretation is so difficult that Sir William Hamilton himself failed and misinterpreted consciousness. All this and more of the kind is said of consciousness by these able men at the same time that they claim that it accompanies all our mental operations, that it is not a separate faculty, as subject to the will, and never deceives us. But if consciousness thus gives immediate knowledge and never deceives us, how is it that all do not agree respecting its deliverances? Sir William Hamilton says we are conscious of an external world, as of the table on which we write. With this Professor Fisher, certainly one of the ablest thinkers of the age, agrees,[1] while Professor Calderwood, as I happen to know, does not, and, if I may mention myself in such a connection, I do not. If the question be how many objects we can think of at once, Dugald Stewart says but one; Hamilton says six; and this certainly is a question to be determined by consciousness. If the question be whether there is a separate volition for every step in walking, Dugald Stewart says, Yes, others say, No. If the question be what a man can evolve out of his inner consciousness, we need not go to Germany for strange answers.

With such diversity of function and of meaning in this fundamental word, how is a beginner in these

[1] See *Princeton Review* for July, 1882.

studies to find his way? Can anything be done to aid him? Perhaps not, but a trial may be made.

Going back to the beginning of intelligence in us, whenever that was, there must have been involved in that the certainty of our own existence. Implicitly at least that existence was known, and it is now generally agreed that in the knowing of it there was a simultaneous knowledge of some modification of the Ego by act or affection, and of the Ego itself. The "Cogito ergo sum" of Descartes is not a logical process, but a mode of stating the simultaneous knowledge by one concrete act of two things, one of which was first in the order of time and the other in the order of nature. We know and must know the being, in knowing the modification. Here, then, we have the knowledge of a modification of our being together with a knowledge of that being, and thus a *consciousness*. There is a knowing by the mind of itself as the subject of its own operations at the same time that it knows, and in knowing, those operations.

In consciousness as thus found, and in that only, do we have the three characteristics that are generally claimed for it. The first of these is, that it must accompany and form a part of every recognized mental act. That consciousness as now defined does this we cannot doubt. Man cannot run away from himself; whatever his thought or feeling or modification may be, he must refer it to himself as its subject. He must know himself as knowing, or feeling, or in some way modified. The second characteristic claimed for consciousness is, that it is infallible. It never deceives us. And certainly there can be no fallibility or deception in the reference by a man of his own states to himself. There is, indeed, a supposition lately made, that perhaps I ought to mention, which would render such a reference deceptive: it is that the modifications are the man, and all the man there is. But this is too absurd to require further notice. The third characteristic claimed for consciousness is, that it is not a separate faculty. This, again, is obviously true of consciousness as above defined; not, as Sir William Hamilton says, because it is inclusive of all the faculties, but because it is not subject to the will, and is equally present in the operation of them all. It is a common consciousness, the same to all men.

Knowing thus by consciousness ourselves as existing, what next? Evidently the knowledge of ourselves as continuing to be the same beings at successive times. Do we know this by consciousness? Yes, says Sir William Hamilton, and others of his school. To me it seems clearly not. We know it by the joint action of consciousness and memory. We know it immediately and necessarily, but not by the action of consciousness alone. Knowing ourselves thus as existing, and as existing permanently, we go on to the truths of reason already mentioned, which all men believe by necessity; and we hold any would be skeptic who would deny them in our grip, by the fact that he must affirm them in action; and by not hesitating to treat him as if he believed them. We next pass to simple intuitions. By these we know truths immediately by what Dr. McCosh calls self-evidence, but the subjects of them are not so incorporated into our constitution that we must believe and act upon them. When attention is called to the question, whether two straight lines can inclose a space, we know at once, that is, it is self-evident, that they cannot; but a man may live a lifetime and not have the question brought before him. Then we come to knowledge from observation. And here we have two great fields, or worlds, — the external and the internal. Of the external we gain knowledge only through the senses. This is the knowledge we are commonly said to gain by observation. Of the internal we also gain our knowledge by what is properly observation, but here our language is at fault. Locke said we gained it by reflection. Hamilton says by *self*-consciousness, thus making no difference between his consciousness and this. He also speaks of an inner sense, which is better. Generally, however, we are now said to gain this knowledge by consciousness, that being defined to be a knowledge by the mind of its own acts and affections. This is the common meaning of the word, and as thus commonly used it is useless to object to it; but it should be understood that the external and the internal field are equally fields of observation, that in both facts are to be noted, compared, and classified, that in doing this the faculties are employed in both under the direction of the will, so that we are liable, and perhaps equally in both, to mistakes; and that in both we reach only classified science as the result of observation. It is a weak point with consciousness as it is now used that it claims a clearness and certainty that many times not only cannot be attained in the field to which it is assigned, but in which there is often the greatest uncertainty and difference of opinion. We hear constantly of the clear light of consciousness, of its infallibility; but if we ask Dr. Mansel how we know that God exists, he says it is by consciousness. Dr. McCosh says, "I have my doubts whether, from a mere idea or principle in the mind, we can argue the existence of the living God. It should proceed, I reckon, mainly in the joint inductive and deductive method." And I agree with Dr. McCosh. Some things in this inner field we know certainly, as we do some things in the outer, but in many things there is in both the greatest uncertainty. If consciousness were what it is claimed to be, the Γνῶθι σεαυτόν of the ancient oracle would amount to nothing. This is true whether we suppose the oracle had in view mental science, or that knowledge of motives which is sought for in Christian self-examination. The infallibility claimed for consciousness would give at once, and of course, all the material needed for mental science, and all the motives needed for the determination of character. If this doctrine had been held in ancient times the prophet would not have put forth, in regard to the deceitful and desperately wicked heart, the despairing question: "Who can know it?" The truth seems to be that the two departments of knowledge — in the one of which we know by necessity, with no act of the will, and with a certainty from which we cannot escape, and that in which we know through attention that may be more or less, and through the voluntary use of our faculties that may or may not be withheld — are so different in their processes and results that the one word consciousness cannot cover both without perplexity and confusion. In connection with some modification of ourselves consciousness may tell us *that* we are, and the affirmation may accompany us, in connection with whatever modification there may be, through our whole lives; but to know *what* we are, through a knowledge of these changing modifications, is wholly another thing. We may know that there is a modification, and know ourselves through that, without knowing what the modification is as distinguished from others. At this point lies the mistake of those who hold to the infallibility of consciousness, and yet define it as a knowledge by the mind of its own operations. They seem to hold that if the mind knows itself in knowing a modification of itself, it must also know distinctively what that modification is. It might seem so, but nothing can be further from the truth. President Porter and Hamilton both say, that in all operations of the mind, intellect, sensibility, and will act together. Perhaps so, but I am not sure of it, as I should be if this doctrine of consciousness were correct. Who shall decide? It seems, therefore, almost like mockery to claim infallibility for the organ of knowledge in a department, the special scandal of which has been its uncertainty.[1]

[1] See Appendix, Note D.

What then have we found? First a *being*, and the knowledge of his own existence by a being who knows himself to be, and can say *I*. This knowledge of himself, which is to accompany him through his whole existence, is his starting point, and places him at once above all material objects, however great, and above the animal creation. It involves *personality*. He can say, I am. I have being, and know myself as having it. In this is consciousness. In this he is in the image of God, who knows Himself as having being, and who reveals Himself as the *I AM*, and the *I AM* that *I AM*,—the being that I know myself to be. All that belongs to personality is involved in this, and will necessarily be revealed when the occasion shall come. He will have a knowledge of rights and of obligation, and so of himself as a moral being; he will have the power of intuition, that is, of rational insight; he will have the power of scientific classification and arrangement, and so the power of bringing all things into a system; and he will have the power of comprehension,—of comprehending ends as subordinate, ultimate, and supreme, even his own end. In all this, so far as a finite being can be, he will be intellectually in the image of God. So far as he is thus in his image he will be able to know Him, to enter into sympathy with Him in his purposes, and to work together with Him for their accomplishment.

In a being thus intellectually constituted and thus able to sympathize with God and to work together with Him, we have, as I think, the Bible idea of man as intellectually in the image of God.

In differing thus radically from the current philosophy, in regard to consciousness, I cannot hope to reform either that philosophy or the language. These must take their course. My object has been to aid you, gentlemen, in your studies, by presenting for your consideration a simpler and more definite working apparatus than the one now generally adopted.

4

III.

KNOWLEDGE CONTINUED. — FEELING. — FREE CAUSATION.

MAN was made to know the truth. It is the Scriptural idea of man that he is not only to know necessary truth, as in the image of God, but that he is also to seek for truth that it costs him labor to obtain. He is to "buy the truth and sell it not." It may be well, therefore, before we pass from the consideration of man as endowed with intellect, and in the image of God through that, to look at some considerations that may guide us in adopting those beliefs that are based on a balance of probabilities, but carry with them a conviction short of certainty. This is the more desirable because it is upon such beliefs that the conduct of life mainly depends. What are the grounds on which we may not, or may, in any case whatever, found a rational belief of this kind?

And first, we may not and cannot believe a contradiction or an absurdity.

A contradiction may be made by two propositions mutually opposed, and then we cannot believe both; or by a single proposition that asserts a union of qualities that we know to be incompatible. We cannot believe that it both rains and does not rain at the same time and place, or that the same figure can be both round and square. From the imperfection of language, it is not always easy to distinguish between a contradiction and a paradox. When the Apostle Paul says of himself that he had nothing and yet possessed all things, it seems to be a contradiction, and yet there is a sense in which it is true. We need, therefore, before pronouncing a proposition to be a contradiction, to be sure that we fully understand the subject, and also that the words, in the connection in which they are used, are susceptible of but a single meaning.

An absurdity is any proposition that is opposed either to a first truth, or to a mathematical axiom or demonstration. No one can believe there can be a body that is not in space, or that the whole is not equal to the sum of its parts.

Second. We are not to believe a proposition unless it is more rational to believe it than not to believe it.

To the extent implied in this proposition I am a rationalist. Rationalist is a good name perverted. As now used, it involves a claim by those who adopt it to be more fully guided by reason than others, and that we do not allow. I believe in reason. I say with Bishop Butler, " Let reason be kept to, but let not such poor creatures as we are go on objecting against an infinite scheme that we do not see the necessity or usefulness of all its parts, and call that reasoning." I believe in the capacity and duty of reason to judge of anything claiming to be a revelation from God. Also, that reason has the capacity to judge, and ought to judge, what is the meaning of anything thus claiming to be a revelation. But when anything has been accepted as a revelation, and its meaning ascertained, then I hold that it is the business of reason, as reason, to believe it. This I hold on the ground that confidence in the God who gave us our faculties ought rationally to be as great as in the faculties themselves. Certainly, if we cannot trust Him, we cannot trust the faculties given by Him. But this rationalism does not say, and I hold that, in saying it, we are more rational than rationalism. As some of old, "professing themselves to be wise, became fools," so we think that rationalists, professing themselves to be rational, become irrational.

Third. We are not to believe what we do not understand.

By this I mean here, that, in order to assent to a proposition, we must know its meaning. This may seem self-evident, but needs to be stated as a guard against nonsense and an indefiniteness that amounts to the same thing. Too often ignorance conceals itself and puts on an air of profoundness, by the use of indefinite terms or of terms in such relation that they convey no definite meaning. When Hegel says, and makes it the starting-point of his system, "thought and being are identical," the words are familiar and the sentence is simple, but it conveys no meaning whatever to my mind. To me, the thinker is, and must be, one thing, and the thought another.

So, too, when Mr. Herbert Spencer says "Life is a continuous adjustment of internal relations to external relations," and asks me if I believe that, I say to him that the boiling of water in a tea-kettle is a continuous adjustment of internal relations to external relations, and ask him if he believes that. The trouble with this definition, which is equally applicable to hearing or seeing, I suspect to be that it does not mean anything at all, and so can neither be believed nor disbelieved. The words are familiar, they are put together grammatically, and so they are when I say that internal relations are to external relations as four to six, but no one can get any meaning from them. If it be said that there is an adjustment of things to things, I understand what is meant; but I do not understand what is meant by an adjustment of relations to relations, nor how an adjustment of these tenuous abstractions can constitute that, whatever it may be, which distinguishes the vast realm of organized from unorganized being. Indeed, I do not understand what is meant by internal relations or external relations, unless it be the relation of internal and external things; and then the definition of life would be a continuous adjustment of the relations of internal things to the relations of external things, — a proposition which I am unable either to believe or to disbelieve. Passages of this kind might be given indefinitely. I will simply add the definition by Hegel, of "the essence as such," as it is given by Schwegler, in a translation by President Seelye, which secures its accuracy: "The essence as reflected being is the reference to itself only as it is the reference to something other." It would be a great gain if writings that claim to be philosophical and profound could be freed from this class of propositions.

Fourth, and positively. It is rational to believe, on evidence, facts the causes and the mode of which we do not understand.

This is what some suppose they mean when they say they will not believe what they do not understand; but they cannot mean that, for there is no man who understands the causes and mode of the larger part of the facts which he believes. No one hesitates to accept the fact of an earthquake or of the aurora borealis who simply knows the fact and nothing more. He does not know the cause or the mode of the fact, but he knows no reason why the fact might not be.

But, fifth. There are facts in connection with which the element of mystery comes in. This comes in in connection with facts which seem inconsistent with all we have previously known. To a child one thing is as wonderful and mysterious as another. He does not know enough to wonder. But when a course of nature has been recognized, and anything occurs that conflicts with our experience, and so conflicts that its cause and mode are inconceivable to us, there is mystery. Here, again, men say they will not believe what they do not understand; but no man can rationally say this if he means that he will not believe on evidence a fact thus related to his understanding. To any man who lived fifty years ago the cause and mode of a communication passing from New York to London in a second or less would be inconceivable, and yet he might have such evidence of the fact that it would be folly not to believe it. So it is with all cases of mystery and of facts not in accordance with what we have known of the order of causation. Any fact that is possible may have such evidence that it would be folly not to believe it; and the men who undertake to say, *a priori*, what facts are and what are not possible in such a universe as this may find, as has happened in some signal instances, that the fact is accomplished while they are demonstrating its impossibility.

Once more. Each of two propositions may be so supported by evidence that it may be rational to believe both, though we cannot reconcile them with each other.

Two statements are made to a man not an astronomer. One is, that the north star is fixed, and that, as he knows by observation, the pole of the earth either does or seems to point equally to it at all seasons of the year. The other statement is, that the earth moves in its orbit round the sun, its axis being parallel with itself, a hundred and eighty millions of miles, the distance being measured in a straight line from one extremity of the orbit to the other. But if this be true, the pole of the earth must be directed at one time in its orbit to a point in space a hundred and eighty millions of miles distant from that to which it was directed at another point, and that would render it apparently impossible that it should either point, or seem to point, equally in all parts of its orbit to one fixed point. With these two statements before him what is the man to do? Is he to say, as I once heard a man who was so far forth a rationalist, say, "The astronomers are mistaken. The star moves, and its motion corresponds to that of the earth. It must be so." Or is he to accept both statements as true on the testimony of astronomers, and suppose that there may be an element in the case of which he is ignorant? In the broadest sense of the word rational, taking into view the strength of the testimony that might be brought, the limitation of his faculties in their relation to a subject so vast, and his lack of previous study, it would be rational to accept both statements and wait till some one should explain to him the effect of distance on parallax, and then he would not only believe both facts, but see how they could be reconciled. This instance is taken from natural science, but occasions for the application of this rule are more frequent in connection with the truths of revelation. Men do not see the consistency of the foreknowledge, or purposes, or decrees of God with human freedom; and so, instead of seeking candidly for the evidence of each, they reject one or the other. They do not see the consistency of the doctrine of the Trinity with the divine Unity, and so they reject one or the other, more commonly that of the Trinity, but sometimes, virtually at least, that of the Unity. Coming up as we do from entire ignorance into a universe so vast and complex as this, we ought to expect, it is folly not to expect, that the evidence for single facts which are so far removed from all we have known before as to be inconceivable to us, and also for each of two facts which we cannot reconcile with each other, may be such that the only rational course will be to accept the facts, and leave the mode of the facts and of their reconciliation to the ampler knowledge of the future.

It is more especially in connection with the last two mentioned propositions that men say they will not believe what they do not understand, meaning by that, that they will not believe a fact the mode of which they cannot conceive of, or which they are unable to reconcile with some other fact. But in saying this they fail to distinguish the processes of the mind when the question, What is? is asked, from those when, How it is? is asked. When the question, What is? is asked, the mind should be governed wholly by evidence. To this there is no limitation, except the avoidance of contradiction or absurdity. Whoever is sure he so comprehends the whole subject that the fact or statement in question can be seen to involve a contradiction or an absurdity cannot believe that statement or fact. Short of that, he is to be governed wholly by evidence. But in strictness the term, understand, does not apply when we deal with evidence of what has been or is, as it does when we inquire *how* it came to be. Was my house entered last night? Yes, I have evidence of it, and know it from the absence of my overcoat, and from tracks on the floor; but *how* it could have been entered I do not understand. If, then, we apply, as we should, the term *know* to facts as proved by evidence, and the term *understand* to modes and causes, there is a sense in which a man may properly say he will not believe what he does not understand, in which, indeed, he cannot believe it. The fact he knows; the evidence for it he knows; of the mode of it he knows nothing and believes nothing.

It ought to be added that if there be modes of being or of action in this universe which we do not share, it would not be rational to suppose that we can conceive of them, much less understand their modes or causes. This we all know is true, even of the senses. If, therefore, there be — as there may be, and doubtless are, in angels or in God — modes of being or perception which we do not share, the fact may be made known to us by testimony; but to suppose that we can conceive of or comprehend them would be opposed to all the laws of thought.

But if we are to believe nothing which it is not more rational to believe than not to believe, what becomes of the conflict between reason and faith? There is no such conflict, there never was, and nothing but perverseness or the most marvelous stupidity could have led to the supposition that there is. The faith required by Christianity is not credulity, it is not belief without evidence. It is wholly rational, and that minister of the gospel who fails to represent it so, is false to his trust. That faith is not simple belief. It is confidence in a person, involving an act of the will, and the belief and confidence involved are never required, except on *sufficient* and *rational* grounds. "Trust ye in the Lord forever, *for* in the Lord Jehovah is everlasting strength." Paul knew whom he had believed, and *therefore* he believed Him. He was persuaded that He was able to keep that which he had committed to Him against that day, and *therefore* he committed it to Him.

We can now see our ground. As endowed with intellect, we have necessary knowledge, and in that all the guard against skepticism that is possible. Not accepting it, man cannot act, or speak, or even think, without a contradiction. It is *knowledge* that we have, and not mere faith or belief. Does any one inquire for the ground of this knowledge? We say that that ground is the authority of the faculties so revealed that we must know it to be their authority. This we also say is the highest authority that we can conceive even God to give. For, look at it: unless we are to accept the authority of our faculties unequivocally expressed, we could never be sure of a revelation, however made, as from God. Having thus necessary knowledge, always coming without effort, we have also knowledge that is gained by effort. Here we *may* have certainty, or we may have mere belief or opinion resting on a preponderance of evidence. In all the operations of the intellect here there is large room for the exercise of the will, and it is a part of the probation of men, with some a large part, to see that there is perfect candor throughout the whole process of reaching such opinions and beliefs. In the exercise of such candor we are to receive on all subjects whatever presents itself as truth or fact for which there is sufficient evidence, and we are to reject, or hold in doubt, everything claiming to be a fact or a truth for which there is not sufficient evidence. In this way the harmony of all truth will follow as fast as truth shall be ascertained and accepted. It can follow in no other way.

We now proceed to inquire in what, besides his intellect, man is in the image of God.

Inseparably connected with the exercise of our intellect we have, generally, if not always, feeling. Are we in this in the image of God? Yes. Nothing can be more opposed to the Scriptural idea of God than the conception of Him as without feeling. Buddhists, Brahmins, Pantheists, may conceive of what they call God as without feeling; philosophers may speculate about the Infinite and the Absolute, and call it God, and say that feeling is incompatible with these ideas; but the Bible knows of no God without feeling. Without that there is no fatherhood, no love, no compassion or mercy; there is no righteousness, or holiness, or justice, no complacency or moral indignation, no moral government. In the Bible idea of God we have feeling as commensurate with his other attributes, and it is a little remarkable that those who speak of infinity, as excluding the idea of feeling, do not see that in excluding that they also exclude the idea of infinity. The same is true of personality which involves other attributes than that of feeling. Personality they speak of as the highest conceivable form of being, and yet as incompatible with infinity, because, as they conceive of it, it implies limitation. But what kind of an infinite being is it that can exist and not manifest himself in the highest conceivable form of being? No idea of limitation can be more incompatible with that of infinity than the absence from it of personality, including the attribute of feeling. In our powers of knowledge we are in the image of God, because we are able in some things and to some extent to know as He knows. And so in feeling we are in his image, because in some things, and to some extent, we are capable of feeling as He feels. Does God love? So can we. Love is more than feeling, but we can have the feeling that enters into that. Does He feel pity, or complacency in goodness, or moral indignation? So, in our measure, can we, and thus, through that capacity of feeling which is among the primitive revelations of a man to himself, are we in the image of God.

Feeling is so incorporated into every form of our activity as to enter into every conception of ourselves. It reveals itself in our capacity for both enjoyment and suffering, and probably the capacity for the one always corresponds to that for the other. The relation of feeling to the will is peculiar. It can never be made the immediate object of choice or volition, and yet there would be no choice or volition without it. If there were no feeling, we should never eat; and yet, in eating, our choice and volition have for their immediate object the food and not the feeling. The feeling is the immediate result of our activity from our being constituted as we are, and never of an act of choice or of will. According to the threefold division now universally prevalent in psychology, feeling is the product of the sensibility. This division, being thus fully accepted, should be fully carried out. This has not been done, and much misapprehension has been the consequence. The system of morals, as I have presented it, has been misapprehended from this cause. Making this distinction fully, so as to refer all feeling to the sensibility, we shall see that *a good*, without some conception of which the will could not act, is the normal product of the sensibility, and that nothing is a good that is not the product of that. Let us see. We study. In connection with the activity of the intellect in that way we have enjoyment, that is, a good, — not because we willed it, but because we are so constituted that, on the condition of our studying, the enjoyment will come without our willing it. In our study we have knowledge for our object, and not enjoyment or a good; but if there were no enjoyment either in the study or from the use of the knowledge acquired, — none either for ourselves or for others, — we should not continue to study. Of course, the enjoyment is originally known through spontaneous or instinctive activity, and afterwards becomes, though not the immediate object of the activity, yet a condition without which it would not be voluntarily entered upon. From this intimate relation of feeling to activity, it is not strange that they should have been so far identified as to be called by the same name, especially when the element of feeling predominates. In study this is not apt to be done. We readily separate our activity in study from the feeling and enjoyment that comes from it. The study, the activity itself, we do not call a good; the feeling, the enjoyment, we do. But as feeling increases, the two become more blended and difficult of separation. Hence, while there is really the same distinction in all forms of virtue and holiness, they being radically forms of activity of the will, they are said to be not only good, but *a* good, and the denial of this is thought to indicate a theory of morals that is to be looked down upon as low, if not to be abhorred as wicked. The sole difference, however, is that while one blends the activity and its result under the one name holiness, and calls that a good, the other separates the two, and calls the result only a good. We thus see how men may seem to be strongly opposed to each other who are yet substantially agreed.

We thus see what feeling is, and its place in our constitution. It may come to us from the action of others, but as the direct result of our own activity and the indirect result of our wills, it becomes a motive to action or a deterrent from it. If the normal result of the activity be one of pleasure, satisfaction, happiness, enjoyment, blessedness, it is *a good*. It has value in itself, — an absolute value. It can be neither exchanged, nor bought, nor sold. It has no utility. It is good for nothing. It is simply *a good*.

In claiming, as we do, affinity with God, through feeling, caution is needed, because there is a wide range of feeling that we have in virtue of our being in the image of that which is below us. It is only through the feelings connected with our moral and spiritual nature that we are, as having feeling, in the image of God.

We now pass on. Having, as we have seen, powers of knowledge, and a sensibility embracing under it the whole range of feeling, what more does man find revealing itself as an essential part of his being, and by which he is in the image of God?

He — that is, the man, the ego — is essentially active, and, if intelligently so, he must choose, and put forth effort to obtain the object of his choice. In doing these, man is revealed to himself as having a personal will, as free, and as a cause. FREEDOM and CAUSATIVE POWER, — in both of these man is in the image of God.

In choice and volition we have the two factors of the will, the constituents of man as a free agent. In the choice he is free, and in the carrying out of the choice, that is, in volition, he is an agent, — so, a *free agent*. This act of choice, in which, if anywhere, freedom is to be found, is one the conditions and nature of which it is of special interest that the minister of the gospel should understand. It is an act in the spiritual realm revealing itself only to the man himself and to God, producing no outward effect, nor, as yet, any effect, except in its reaction on the agent; yet by this act he may put himself in an attitude toward God or his fellow-men from which may flow the efforts of a lifetime, or, if he is restrained from making effort, his position morally will be the same as if he had done so. The act is simple, and enters as an element into man's life as necessarily as thought. As between two things, he may be free to choose either, but he is not free whether he will choose. He may say he will not choose either of those things, but he can say that only by a choice to choose neither. We may, therefore, say that *a* choice is necessitated, but that *the* choice is free. As simple, the act of choice cannot be defined. No one who has not done it can be told what it is. As simple, too, and immediate, it is done without means, and therefore no one can tell another *how* to do it. He may tell him which of two objects to choose, but if the man says he does not know how to perform the act of choice, he cannot tell him that. The inquiry, How? always has reference to the use of means. If there be no means there can be no how. An excuse, too, for not doing a required act always lies in the region of means. An absolute want of means for an act requiring them is a valid excuse, but if the man have the means, the only reason that can be given for not doing it is that he did not choose to do it; and that, if the required act was a duty, is no excuse. It involves and necessitates a direct conflict of will with the authority requiring the act.

By thus placing freedom, and so moral responsibility, in a region where no means are required, God has secured two things. The first is that the character, and so the destiny, of every man is so put into his own hands that no human power can reach or interfere with it. Here we have the possibility and grandeur of a rational martyrdom. The choice to obey God rather than man abides. The flames cannot reach it, and the moment of their conquest over the body is the moment of the martyr's conquest over all the powers that earth can bring to shake his allegiance to God and to duty. The second thing secured by placing freedom where no means are required is the impossibility of any excuse before God for not obeying any of his commands. His command is to love, and as the central act of love is choice, there can be nothing but a want of will in the way, and so no excuse.

The condition or prerequisite of choice is an alternative presented. This may be between two objects, either but not both of which he may have, or between two courses of action, either but not both of which he may take. This limits the range of human freedom. Practically, the range of choice, and so of freedom for man, is limited to those things which it is possible for him to attain or to do. A man may choose between walking and riding, but not between walking and flying. Freedom is also practically limited by the alternatives presented. Having the offer of his expenses and a journey to Europe, a young man may choose whether he will accept it, but whether he shall have the offer is not a matter of choice.

But whatever may be the conditions or limitations of choice they do not affect its freedom. The knowledge of this by man I place on the same basis in regard to certainty as the knowledge of his existence. This I do, because the idea of freedom is a necessary product of his faculties in connection with choice, and the fact of freedom in choosing is necessarily known. It is so known, because the man cannot deny it in words without contradicting it in action; because, if a man do deny it in words we treat him, and have a right to treat him, as if he believed it; and because the fact of freedom can no more be proved by anything plainer than itself than the fact of our existence.

As choice and freedom are wholly in the spiritual realm, and need not express themselves outwardly, nothing can interfere with them unless it be something in that realm that precedes them. That which precedes them is what have been called motives, and the controversy, in regard to freedom, has turned chiefly on the influence of these. Man, it has been persistently said, is under a necessity of choosing in accordance with the strongest motive, and such necessity is, of course, incompatible with freedom. If this be so, there can be no freedom for either God or man, since there can be no choice or freedom unless there be an alternative with what are called motives on each side. Perhaps we have no more signal instance of the reaction of words upon thought than is found in these two — *motive* and *strongest*. The words are unfortunate. There is in them, or rather in the things signified by them, neither motive power nor strength. The plain statement of the case, and all that can be said about it, is that grounds, inducements, reasons for action in different directions are placed before men, that they deliberate respecting these, and then choose. *They* act, and nothing else does. They move themselves, and there is no strength or moving power out of themselves. Certainly there is nothing, either out of themselves or in themselves, that is not necessary as a condition of freedom.

Choice being a free act suffices to reveal character before God. "Forasmuch as it was in thine heart," said God to David, "to build me an house, thou didst well that it was in thine heart." The choice, the will, was accepted for the deed. But man would not be as fully as now in the image of God if he had not the power to carry out his choices in action, and to realize in outward form those conceptions and ideals on which the choices were based. This he does by *volition*, the second factor of what is called will. Through this it is that he reveals both character and causative power to his fellow-men. There may be choice without volition, but not volition without choice; for, however long the choice may abide, holding the volition, or executive act, in abeyance, yet that act can never be without an immediately preceding choice. But while volition may be thus separated from choice, they are naturally conjoined, and are originally known as a single act. It is through them, as thus conjoined, that I suppose we have by necessity the idea of causation, and of ourselves as causes. Without energy put forth by us, followed by results, and immediately known by us as cause and effect, I do not see how it would be possible for us to have the conception of anything in the ongoing of nature, but of antecedent and consequent. The search for causes which has been so universal could never have been thought of, and all the philosophy possible would have been what Comte conceived it to be, the discovery and record of a stated order. This would, of course, apply to mind as well as to matter, and would reduce everything to mere mechanism and fatalism.

As the idea of a cause and of causation thus necessarily arises in the putting forth of energy by us, it seems to me both unphilosophical and unfortunate to bring in other elements as going to constitute the idea. An agent putting forth power, with results following, is what every one understands. He is a cause, and the results are effects; and to call anything a cause that has not in it this original element of energy, is simply to make the word ambiguous. A cause is that which so puts forth energy as to produce a change. That is a cause, and nothing else is. Of course, the word has secondary meanings. It may also be allowed, but is undesirable, that it should be used in another sense, with an adjective prefixed, as final cause, in which there is no resemblance or analogy to a cause in its original meaning; but when cause is defined, as by Hamilton, as involving "the absolute tautology between the effect and its causes," the idea of energy becomes simply that of transmutation, and pantheism must inevitably follow. There could be no such thing as sin unless it had been eternal. Besides, in some of its applications, this doctrine that there can be nothing in the effect that was not in its causes becomes unintelligible. Ice is melted by heat. Does it mean anything to say that the melting was in the heat? Is the drunkenness caused by rum in the rum? Is the destruction caused by a tornado in the tornado? Was there destruction there before it struck its object? There was in it power, energy, force; that we know, and it is all that we know. There is no tautology. That which originally gave the idea of causation is necessarily there, and nothing else is. We should naturally suppose that there would be in that which originally gives us the idea, all there is that is essential in the idea. And so it is. It is with this as with all products of similar origin. The same idea of being that was originally given accompanies us in all our thinking; also the same idea of personal identity; and so of causation, and of ourselves as causes. If, as Hamilton holds, this idea or principle of causation was an original datum of our constitution, this, as it seems to me, must be so.

But there is another definition of cause given by Hamilton, in which he and Mill are agreed; and as Voltaire said of an Englishman and a Frenchman, that when they agree in anything we may be sure they are right, so we should suppose it might be said of Hamilton and Mill, generally so antagonistic. The definition is this: "By cause I mean everything without which the effect could not be realized." This definition has been adopted and defended by able thinkers in this country, but to me it seems not only incompatible with the fact, that the principle of causation is an original datum of our constitution, always going with us, so that we cannot move or speak without involving it, but also incompatible with clearness of thought, or precision of language. According to this, the battle-field and the sunlight without which the battle could not have been fought, are a part of the cause of the battle; the ocean is a part of the cause of the falls of Niagara. But for the bush, behind which he was concealed, and his gun, the assassin could not have committed the murder; and so the bush and the gun were a part of the cause, and might be called on to share the responsibility. Who but a philosopher ever supposed that the foundation of a house was a part of the cause of the house? The common people and common language make a distinction between the foundation of a house and its builder. The one they call a condition, or prerequisite, and the other a cause, and they are right. Who can suppose that space is a cause, or part of the cause, of motion? The doctrine, as stated by Hamilton, and especially by Mill, with whom it seems to have originated, amounts to this: that the possibility of an event is in all cases a part of the cause of that event. The possibility that a man should lift a weight is a condition of his lifting it; but to make it a part of the cause would not only be contrary to usage, which gives law to language, but would give an extension to the word, cause, that would unfit it for use in philosophical discussions. The condition of any event being its possibility, everything involved in that possibility will be a part of the condition, and so of the causes. According to that, the cause of our being here to-day could not be ascertained without going back at least to the discovery of this country by Columbus. All change requires a cause. As I have said, any exertion or manifestation of energy that produces a change is a cause, and, as I think, nothing else should be so called. It is here, as in consciousness. The inwrought element of our constitution, with its necessitated product, by which we are in the image of God, has become blended with others of a different origin, so that it is impossible to argue, or even to think successfully, with a word that carries in its meaning elements so diverse.

As free then, and as a cause, man is in the image of God. He is as free as a rational being can be conceived to be. Does he, when an alternative is presented, with reasons on either side, choose in view of those reasons? Does *he* do it? If so, he is free. If not, freedom is impossible. Does he, again, when anything is to be done, understandingly, and with reference to an end, originate motion? If so, he is a cause, and a first cause. A second cause is necessitated by a previous one. A first cause originates the movement. If man has not the power to originate his own movements, if it is not he who originates the movement of his lips when he speaks, then he is not a cause at all.

Having thus freedom and the power of causation, there is a sense in which man is in the image of God as a creator. Place a being thus free, having the power of causation, and with intelligence, in the midst of a fixed order of things so that he can foreknow what the consequences of his acts will be, and it is plain that he can purposely and intelligently create, or cause to be, a future that, but for him, would not have been. Feeble as is this image of the creative power of God, it yet indicates for man a place in this universe higher than that of suns and stars. He is not wholly as the driftwood on the stream or the atom in the whirlwind, atom though he be, but he has a will that goes for something in that which is to be.

IV.

THE MORAL NATURE.

INTELLECT, Sensibility, Will, these we have found in the necessitated revelation of man to himself, but we have not yet found all that is thus necessarily revealed, nor all by which we are in the image of God. We have not found all that is requisite for personality. For that, and for the full image of God, we need the Moral Nature. Whether there could be Intellect, Sensibility, and Will without that, I do not know, but certainly there could not be personality. A being without rights, and not under obligation, could not be a person.

Rights and Obligation,— in these we find the primitive manifestations of the Moral Nature. We have Rights first, and Obligation as the reciprocal of Rights. These inhere in the person, and are necessarily known in connection with conduct that relates to the well-being of ourselves or others. A man as necessarily knows that he has a right to himself in the unobstructed use of his faculties, when he does not interfere with the rights of others, as he knows his personal identity. With the same necessity he knows, when he comes into intelligent relation to other beings, that he is under obligation to do some things and to abstain from doing others. This must be so if man has a moral nature, because we mean by a nature that which, in given circumstances, will produce a uniform result. Uniformly, the conditions being given, men have a knowledge of Rights and of Obligation, and so may properly be said to have a Moral Nature.

This nature, with its revelations and results in the sensibility, is central, and, as central, is the last element to be revealed. It is the blossom at the centre of the palm tree, to the guarding and unfolding of which all the other parts conspire, and through which alone we reach a knowledge of its highest possibilities, and so of its end. The highest end of man is to be found in and from a full display of intelligent agency in connection with his rights and his obligations.

In considering our causative power, we found it revealing itself in two branches. By the one, which we call the power of choice, we are able to produce changes within ourselves, and to place ourselves in new moral relations; by the other, which we call volition, we are able to produce changes in the external world. So, also, do we now find the Moral Nature revealing itself in two branches, the one relating to ourselves as having rights, the other relating to others as having not only rights, but capacities for well-being and the reverse. As having his own rights which he is to guard, and as the appointed guardian of the rights of those under him, man was created in the image of God. God has rights. He guards them. He violates no right, and suffers no right to be violated without an expression of his displeasure. In this is his perfect righteousness.

And not only has man rights, he is also under obligation. He is under obligation to others, not only as they have rights, and as obligation is the reciprocal of rights, but as they have capacities for well-being which he is bound to promote. He is thus in the image of God as having a capacity for holy love.

Rights and obligation, as I have said, pertain to the person. Right pertains to actions and to conduct. As thus used, the word *right* has two senses. In the one it means conducive to the end in view, whether that be good or bad. In the other it means morally right. In the first sense the word indicates a quality inherent in the thing to which it is applied, as the right road, the right rule. The road, the rule, the act, the conduct, is conducive to the end in view. In the second sense the word is wholly figurative and does not express a quality in the thing to which it is applied. This we see the moment we analyze our thought, and yet there has been a general and most misleading impression that acts and conduct have inherent in themselves a moral quality. But evidently there is no more a moral quality in what is called a moral act than there is a criminal quality in what is called a criminal court, or a joyful quality in what is called a joyful occasion. The morality, the criminality, the joyfulness, can be only in persons. Hence, while the meaning of the word right, in its first sense, expresses the quality of an act as conducive to an end to which we look forward, its meaning in the second sense is expressive, not of any quality in the act itself, but of the source of the act to which we look back. There is, then, and can be, no moral quality in an act, or in conduct, or in things, or in the nature of things. Morality has to do wholly with persons, and hence, in speaking of man as having a moral nature, I have spoken of rights and of obligation which enter into our conception of his personality rather than of an abstract idea of right that can belong only to the intellect, or to right which can belong only to conduct, and that in a figurative way.

As a condition for the fundamental ideas of rights and of obligation, and, indeed, of any moral idea, there must be a Sensibility that will give us, in some form, *a good*. A good is that which has value in itself. It must be subjective. Nothing without us can have other than a relative value, — can be a good. Pleasure, happiness, satisfaction, joy, blessedness, — these and their equivalents are all from the sensibility. Each is a good, has value in itself, — small, it may be, but still, value. Without the idea of a good in some form the will could not rationally act. Generally the will acts in view of something regarded as good, rather than as a good, because, as I have shown, a good can never be the direct object or product of an act of the will; but if there were not a good, there could be nothing good with reference to which the will could act. Without this idea, rights can have no meaning. A right cannot attach itself to anything that has not value, real or supposed, absolute or relative, actual or possible, and value has no significance except with reference to a good of ourselves or some one else. And as rights have relation to our own capacity for good, so does obligation to others have relation to their capacity for good. If they had no capacity for good of any kind, they could have no rights, and we could not be under obligation to them.

The fact, just noticed, that the Moral Nature appears later in the order of time than the Sensibility, and is conditioned upon it, does not indicate its inferiority, but the reverse. In all the upbuilding of nature the conditioning is lower than that which is conditioned upon it.

We have now found the elements involved in personality. We have found man in the image of God as capable of knowledge and of rational comprehension. According to his measure he knows as God knows. We have found him in the image of God in his capacity for feeling, and for the same order of feelings that God has. We have found him in the image of God as capable of choosing freely between different principles of action, and so, different ends, and of carrying out his choices intelligently and purposely so as, in an important sense, to create a future. We have also found him in the image of God as a moral being, as having rights, and as capable through the law of obligation of becoming a law unto himself. Through these it is that man comes to the knowledge of himself as a person; as having dignity and worth, and a capacity for worthiness, and that he is able, in the fullness of its meaning, to say *I*. These are not the *I*, the Ego, the person. They are phenomena through which the person is known to himself as a person, but he is more than they. They are phenomena; he is *Being*.

Now, in thus constructing the person, we have, as I think, a distinct field of knowledge that requires to be more fully separated from others than it has been, and more fully explored if we are to cultivate those others with success. The field is separate as relating to the constitution of the being who is to know all things else. Before we can have science or logic we must have, not only the material, but a being capable of the processes they involve; and I hold that a knowledge of those essential powers, by which such a being is revealed to himself, and without which he would not be a person, must be immediate and necessary, gained by no intervention of the will, and so by nothing that can properly be called a faculty. The man may not be able to discriminate these powers perfectly, or to state them explicitly, may even deny their existence in words; but they are so inwrought into the texture of his being that his actions must affirm them, and that we shall have a right to treat him as having them. In this knowledge we have nothing that can properly be called science. We have no logic, no induction or deduction. We have the fixed point, or rather centre, in the whirlwind of conflicting theories and logical formulas, which is not the whirlwind, but without which that could not be.

What name we may give to the power by which we thus know the essential powers and characteristics of our being as persons, is not so important. Some may think, and perhaps justly, that it would be better to extend the term consciousness over this whole field of necessary knowledge rather than limit it, as I have suggested, to the knowledge of our own existence. To this I now see no objection, and in it some advantages. I see no objection to saying that in knowing my own being through the operation of those powers that constitute my personality, I must know, implicitly at least, those operations and powers as distinguished from others.

Of the person as thus found the aspects are three. The first is, that of a knower. The second is, that of a doer,—an intelligent, comprehending chooser and doer. The third is, that of a being doing what he does under moral law. A being not having these characteristics would not be man. They are the elements which fit man for agency and dominion, and give us, not the whole of the Scriptural idea of man, but a part, the spiritual part, of that double nature which the Scriptures recognize. "For I delight," says the Apostle Paul, "in the law of God after the inward man." Here we have the I, the person, as distinct from the law and delighting in it by approval, as all men must. This law is the law of righteousness and of holiness, of which I have spoken, and which springs directly from that knowledge of rights and of obligation which we have by necessity. In this law that was after the inward man, the Apostle delighted; but he goes on to say: "I see another law in my members warring against the law of my mind, and bringing me into captivity to the law of sin, which is in my members." Here we have the recognition by a being who is fitted to govern, and who calls himself *I*, of a law within him by which he ought to be governed, and also of a law of sin in his members which is opposed to this law. What then are these members? What was it in the original constitution of our nature that needed to be governed?

Man having been fully constituted, that in him which needed to be governed was his spontaneities of thought, of feeling, of impulses, and active principles. By some, spontaneity and choice have been confounded. They are wholly different. Spontaneity, that is, original spontaneity, is from the nature, and is without deliberation or choice. Hence we are responsible only for its control. "Be ye angry and sin not." The anger is spontaneous, but, take care. The spontaneities that we now need to consider are the impulses and principles of action, as the appetites and desires. They involve feeling, without which there could be no motive to action. They are revealed to us, not so much as going to constitute the person, but rather as that which the person, being constituted, is to govern. Still they are so a part of the whole man, that without them the person would have no sphere of action. They are as the subjects in a government. As subjects they are no part of the government, but there could be no government without them. They are of different orders. Some are dependent on the body; some, like the lower branches of the pine that are destined to drop off as the tree rises, are adapted only to the relations of time; and some are fitted for a being capable of an endless existence, and of harmonious relations with God and his whole intelligent universe.

Having these we have the whole man. We have an intelligent agent, under moral law, with freedom of choice, with principles of action between which he is to choose, and with power of outward control.

We now reach a point of transition. Man thus constituted is to *act*, and our next inquiry is, How? This inquiry is answered in the Scriptures, but we wish to know if there is any indication in the structure of his powers, and in their relation to each other, of the mode in which he ought to act. Is there so far an analogy between his structure and a machine that we can see what relation of its parts was intended by its Maker, and would produce the best results? This is the next inquiry in order; but before proceeding to it, I ask your attention to the difference between a principle of action and a law of action. This I do, because the conscience which gives the law of action has been almost universally placed among the principles of action, and has been regarded as differing from them only as having a different object, and as being higher and more authoritative.

A principle of action is that which leads us to act. It supposes an object set over against it which corresponds to it, and in the attainment and possession of which it becomes satisfied, or, at least, finds *a* good. Hunger is such a principle, having food set over against it as its object, and leading to activity in its pursuit, with scope for choice among different kinds of food. The desire for knowledge is such a principle, having knowledge for its object, and leading to activity in its pursuit, with scope for choice among the different departments of knowledge. The man must therefore act sometimes, in choosing, between different principles of action, one that shall be paramount; or, having chosen this principle, in choosing particular objects or lines of action under it. Now, it is among these principles of action that conscience is supposed to have its place, and over against it, as its object, is placed the idea of right. As I have said, conscience is supposed to be the highest and most authoritative of these principles, and the choice of that as supreme to be the sum of duty and the highest form of human action.

A principle of action being thus that which leads us to choose and to act, a law of action should be, and I suppose is, that which directs us how to choose and to act. And as conscience is that from which the law proceeds, and as law can be addressed only to a person, it follows that conscience, instead of having an object before it with reference to which it can act and find its satisfaction, must act directly on the will, or, rather, on the man himself, directing him how to choose and to act. It presupposes grounds of choice and of action. In all cases of moral action, and as a condition for it, there must be an alternative, with grounds for choice and action on either side. A choice may then be made, either between two principles of action, or between two objects or courses of action under the same principle. Here it is, as I suppose, that the voice of conscience comes in, uttered directly to the person, the agent, the man himself, with its imperative ought, or ought not, thou shalt, or thou shalt not. It does not itself present or find an object, but comes in with its imperative, by a voice as from behind and from above, directing us how to choose, saying, "This is the way, walk ye in it."

We now proceed to the question, How is man to act? and the answer to this may possibly enable us to reconcile conflicting views.

In answering this question, philosophers have supposed it necessary for him to choose between different ends of action, but they have differed as to what the end ought to be. Some have said perfection, some virtue or right, some worthiness, some happiness, some blessedness, some the glory of God. Whewell, for example, says, " The supreme object of human action is happiness. Happiness is the object of human action contemplated in its most general form and approved by reason." This he says though he did not regard himself and is not regarded as belonging to the utilitarian school. But this is spoken of by a large class of writers with scorn, as compromising the dignity of our nature. Hear Carlyle: " There is in man a higher than love of happiness. We can do without happiness, and instead thereof find blessedness. Was it not to preach forth this same higher that sages and martyrs, the poet and the priest, in all times have spoken and suffered, bearing testimony through life and through death to the godlike that is in man, and how in the godlike only has he strength and freedom?" In the same way Dr. Charles Hodge opposes happiness to good. He says, "This whole theory is founded on the assumption that happiness is the highest end, and that the desire of happiness is the ultimate spring of all voluntary action. As both these principles are abhorrent to the great mass of cultivated and especially of Christian minds, as men act from other and higher motives than a desire to promote their own happiness, there are few in our day who will adopt the doctrine that the will is as the greatest apparent good as thus expounded. If, however, the word good be taken in a more comprehensive sense, as including everything that is desirable, whether as right, becoming, or useful, then the doctrine is no doubt true. The will, in point of fact, always is determined in favor of that which, under some aspect, or for some reason, is regarded as good. Otherwise, men might choose evil as evil, which would violate a fundamental law of all rational and sensuous natures." Carlyle would permit us to pursue blessedness, and Dr. Hodge good, in some form. The latter says we must do that if we are to act at all, but they both reject strongly, and I suppose Whewell would also, the pursuit of one's own happiness as a paramount principle of action.

Whether the real disagreement here and in similar cases would be as great as it seems if the terms were understood alike, may be questioned. I think not. But if the distinction drawn between principles of action and a law of action be correct, we shall be led to inquire what those principles are, how they are related to each other, and whether our choice should not be made rather between principles of action than between ends of action. Possibly, in doing this, conflicting views may be reconciled.

We have, then, first, what are called the impulsive principles of action. These are the Appetites, the Instincts, the Desires, and the Natural Affections. These act spontaneously on the presentation of their objects, with no intervention of the Intellect or the Will. These principles do not take the name of their object, as their action is called forth by specific objects. Originally, the appetite in us, as in the brute, seeks some single object, not food. That is a general term, of which the brute could know nothing. So the desire of property is primarily the desire of some particular thing; but by combination with the Intellect, it takes its general form, and in that form becomes intensified. That these principles should have acted spontaneously was necessary, for otherwise their objects could never have become motives to us.

The rational principles of action are a regard for rights, self-love, and moral love. These are conditioned on those that are spontaneous. They involve a comparison of the different principles of action and forms of good possible to us, and a choice between them of that which seems best, on the whole, for ourselves and others. The difference between these and the spontaneous principles of action is that the spontaneous act without the intellect and without choice, whereas, in these, both are involved. Except through a comprehension of different forms of good, and through a choice between them, it is impossible that there should be either self-love or a rational and moral love of others.

These principles of action are higher and lower, according to the law of conditioning and conditioned. That is a test of their rank, but the knowledge of that rank cannot be from the intellect alone, through a knowledge of the law. There is connected with it a sentiment that is immediate and intuitive. This, some — as Mr. Martineau — attribute to the Moral Nature, but to me it seems a prerequisite to the action of that nature. As I have said elsewhere, "It is only by the possession and exercise of noble faculties that man comes to a sense of dignity, and in such exercise he comes to it intuitively. No one who has not come to it thus can tell another, or be told, what it is. And as the sense of dignity is thus known, so is the relative dignity of the different powers and of their products. This intuitive perception of an order of the powers [and the same may be said of the principles of action] as higher and lower, and of the corresponding quality of the good from them, is peculiar to man, and is a marked distinction between him and the brutes."

Of these principles, each is good in its place, and, in its normal action, gives us *a* good corresponding in its quality to the rank of the principle. If the principle be one common to us and the brutes, the good from it will be similar to theirs. If it be from one common to us and the angels, the good will be similar to theirs. What the normal action of each of these principles is will be determined by the Law of Limitation. It must be such as will best promote the normal activity of all that is above it. This will be so till we reach the highest principle, and then, as there is nothing above that to limit it, it cannot be in excess. Of course there will be from this the highest quality of good, and the quantity will be in proportion to the activity. The lowest principle of action is Appetite, the highest is Moral Love.

As each of these principles is good in its place, it is not selfish to act from any one of them under the Law of Limitation. The appetites are not selfish. None of the impulsive principles are. They are constitutional principles, and may be made subservient to benevolence as readily as to selfishness. In the only sense in which any act can be disinterested there may be disinterested hate as well as disinterested benevolence. Disinterestedness does not imply that we are uninterested, but only that our interest terminates directly in the good of others. If, however, any one of these principles, lower than the highest, is made supreme, it will involve radical selfishness, will necessitate selfishness in action, and will lead on to any form and degree of wickedness that may be necessary to secure its end.

Of these principles it is necessary that some one should be held as supreme at any given moment. When any one is thus held permanently it determines the character. He who permanently holds, as supreme, the love of money is a miser. That is his character. He who thus holds the love of power is ambitious; and he who thus holds the love of God and his neighbor is religious. This choice of a principle of action as supreme is what is called a generic choice, as it draws after it a great number of particular choices. Those who choose the same active principle, as supreme, are similar in their character; though, from the diversity of lines of action possible under the same active principle, they may be seemingly most diverse.

With these principles, thus arranged, we have conscience revealing and affirming obligation. In all cases of conflict between two of these principles of action, conscience affirms obligation to choose the higher. It also affirms obligation to make the highest supreme.

We have thus Impulsive principles of action, Rational principles, and a Moral imperative. What we need further is the efficient power. This is the man himself, the Person, with freedom and dominion. In a sense the man may be said to be constituted by his powers; but, as I have said, he is more than they. He is a being possessed of powers. He is possessed of Intellect, and Sensibility, and Will, and a Moral nature. He is capable of standing above them, and of comprehending and controlling them. Harm has been done by speaking of the faculties, and especially of the Will, abstractly, as if the Will had a separate existence and was an agent. There is no agent, and no governing power but man. He is the king, capable of ruling, and bound to rule his own spirit. He is also capable of giving himself up to be ruled by the impulsive principles of action. He can choose, in opposition to the counsels of reason and to the commands of conscience, and can give himself up to the commission of wickedness.

Our next inquiry is, What would be the individual and social results if man, knowing himself to be thus constituted, would adopt the highest principle of action as supreme, and would act from the others in accordance with the law of limitation?

In determining this we need to know how a good of any kind comes to us, and the different forms of it of which we are capable.

A good, being always subjective, must be the result of some form of activity. If there be no activity, there can be no knowledge, no virtue, no pleasure or pain, no fatigue or rest, no good or evil. Absolute inactivity is death.

The forms and kinds of a good possible to us are as many as the forms and kinds of activity of which we are capable. By the beneficence of God there is connected, as its result, with every legitimate form of activity, a good. Of the general forms of activity, from which a good may thus result, there are four. The first is from vital action, the involuntary activity of our physical organism. We have from this, when in perfect health, and so far as we are in health, a nameless good which is not a specific sensation, but is better than that, and which is the result of harmonious organic action. It is an undertoned accompaniment of health that constantly speaks of physical well-being.

A second form and quality of good is by a movement from without inward through what are called the afferent nerves. This gives us simple sensation when the object appropriate to the sense is present to it. This comes through each of the five senses, and the form of good thus coming is commonly called pleasure. "It is a pleasant thing to behold the sun." But simple sensation is the least part of the good that comes to us through the senses. There is in the objects presented by some of them, order, proportion, beauty, harmony, grandeur, and thus external nature, with its land and water, mountain and valley, its sun-settings and its sun-risings, and the vault of heaven, is made tributary to our good. In the same way we receive pleasure from the fine arts. The good is from that which enters through the senses, but it needs to be carried up to the Intellect before it can be appreciated and enjoyed. There is no appeal to the conscience or the will. We may or may not need the will to bring us into right relation to the objects, but being in that relation the good comes of itself. What shall we call this good, together with that from simple sensation? It is a just complaint, made by Sir William Hamilton, that the terms in our language to express the forms and results of the

Sensibility are indefinite and inadequate; but I think that, to express the good now spoken of, the term pleasure is commonly used. It is used more widely, but generally, I think, for a form of good that comes by an action that is from without inward, so that in the enjoyment we are relatively passive. Rightly subordinated, the good that may be thus received is great, and is to be thankfully accepted.

The third form of good is from the activity of the impulsive principles of action, as the Desires and the Natural Affections. The objects of these can be obtained only through the activity of the will, causing a movement from within outwards, by means of the efferent nerves. When the will causes a movement from within outward, if the principle of action, whatever it may be, a desire or an affection, comes to rest in the possession of its object, there is a good that is commonly called happiness. Whoever attains by active effort the objects that call into play his natural principles of action is said to be successful and happy. As thus used, the word happiness expresses a good that is the immediate outcome of the unobstructed and successful activity of the powers in the pursuit and possession of their appropriate objects. It is different in its quality from pleasure, and is higher than that.

A fourth form of good will be that in which the Will is brought into activity through the rational principles of action and the conscience. If we suppose that to be done, and the Will, or the Man, to act in accordance with these, he must choose the highest principle of action, whatever that may be, as supreme, and subordinate the others in accordance with the law of Limitation. He can never suffer one that is lower to act except in subordination to that which is higher, and having now a law in the supremacy of the highest, he can never suffer a higher to act so as to encroach on the legitimate province of one that is lower. What the highest principle is, is to be found by a fair analysis of the constitution of man. Let that analysis be made as searching as it may, and I have no doubt it will be found to be the utterance of the constitution no less than of the word of God, that that principle is the *Love of God with all the heart, and of our neighbor as ourselves.* Thus do we identify philosophy with religion.

Let now a man obey his conscience in adopting this principle of action as supreme, and in applying it in the several relations in life, and we shall readily see how his whole nature, as active, will be brought into play, and what the result will be. There will be full scope for the activity of every lower principle of action in its place. There will be the voice of reason and of conscience requiring that act of choice which is central in moral love, and there will be volition bringing into activity the whole man for the attainment of the end proposed by love. Let then the end be attained, and there will be a rational joy from the congruity between the powers and their objects when attained. There will be the approval of conscience, also the consciousness of dignity and worth in the possession and exercise of such powers for such an end; and also an ineffable sense of spiritual well-being, analogous to that of physical well-being, from perfect health. Taken together these will constitute *blessedness*. The godlike in it is from the rational, and especially from the Moral Nature.

The blessedness thus attained will be modified by the character of the beings loved, and by the result of our efforts in their behalf. There is a prevalent impression that love is a mere feeling, drawn out by the excellence of the being loved, but that is not the love commanded in the Bible. The centre of that love is in the Will. It is never consummated, never comes to be, till there is a supreme act of choice by which we commit ourselves to labor, and suffer, if need be, for the good of others. Those others may have excellences of character, or they may not, but they must have capabilities. There must be to them a possibility of good. Having this, want of excellence will not destroy the obligation to love them. So God loves us. So we are to love our enemies. We are not only to love the happy and the good, but also those who are the proper objects of both pity and blame. Loving such, and even failing in our efforts for them, there will still be blessedness, but not that which is perfect. That can be only when the objects of love are of perfect excellence, so that the love of a perfect complacency shall blend with a perfect moral love. This is the highest conceivable form of activity, and from it there must come the highest conceivable form of good.

And here we may see, as we need to see, just how

it may come to pass through disorder in our own nature, and in the world around us, that if we would attain blessedness it must be by a struggle, and that to attain it may require a rejection of all the lower forms of good. Selfishness in ourselves must be eliminated, and, in sympathy with Christ, we must carry on an aggressive warfare with all evil. To do this faithfully must bring self-denial; it may bring martyrdom; but, so doing, if we lose our lives, we shall save them. This is the one thing that we need, and if any are seeking a lower end, and misfortunes lead them to seek blessedness, they will be blessings. This is what Carlyle says in the passage immediately following that quoted in the former part of this lecture. Speaking of the doctrine that in the godlike only has man strength and freedom, he says: "Which God-inspired doctrine art thou too honored to be taught, oh, heavens! and broken by manifold merciful afflictions, even till thou become contrite and learn it. Oh, thank thy destiny for these; thankfully bear what yet remains; thou hast need of them; the self in thee needed to be annihilated. By benignant fever paroxysms is life rooting out the deep-seated chronic disease, and triumphs over death. On the roaring billows of time thou art not ingulfed, but borne aloft into the azure of eternity. Love not pleasure; love God. This is the everlasting yea, wherein all contradiction is solved; wherein whoso walks and works it shall be well with him," — with all which I agree, so far as I understand it, and bating that affectation of style, and of Germanism, into which it is a pity Carlyle ever fell.

So far, I have spoken only of results to the individual. To him those results must be blessedness, together with so much of the lower forms of good as is compatible with that. Of the social results, this is not the place to speak at large. Suffice it to say, that it is too obvious to need proof that we should thus have, as in no other way, the material for a perfect society.

Having thus seen what would follow from choosing, as supreme, the highest principle of action rather than an object of action, we inquire how far we should thus attain each of the objects proposed by philosophers, and so harmonize their systems. Take perfection. Can we conceive of that in man, except as he obeys his conscience in taking the highest principle of action, as supreme, and duly subordinates all others? Is the man perfect who loves God with all his heart, and his neighbor as himself? Is any one perfect who does not? Take virtue. What higher conception of that can we have than that, at every point of a man's life, his conscience should demand, and he should render, that love which is the fulfilling of the law? How, but by such obedience to conscience and such love, can a man attain more of worthiness? How, except from the activity of our highest principle of action in conformity with the law of our being, is blessedness possible? How, with such activity, can it fail to be? How, except in connection with such blessedness, can we expect either pleasure or happiness that will be permanent?

Shall we then say, turning from the speculations of

philosophers, that simply by adopting rationally and conscientiously, as supreme, the principle of action required by the Scriptures, all the ends proposed by those philosophers, whether individual or social, would be gained? So it would appear, and so do we harmonize their systems.

It only remains to say, that as we get the Scriptural idea of man, as in the image of God through the powers given us by Him that are like his own, so do we get the Scriptural idea of him as in the moral image of God through the activity of those powers in accordance with his law, which is also their law. Thus was Adam, and thus is every man, capable of being in the image of God "in righteousness and true holiness."

V.

MAN AS HAVING DOMINION. — AS MALE AND FEMALE.

MAN was made in the image of God, by the creative act of God. "In the image of God made He him." He was in that image when he was created. Of course, all true conceptions of God, so far as man is in his image, must be anthropomorphic.

The powers in virtue of which man is in the image of God are his rational and moral powers, and freedom, or the power of rational choice. These are in their order as lower and higher, but all are essential to personality.

The rational powers include not merely intelligence in a single line, but comprehension. They include the power to comprehend systems as the parts are related to each other and to the whole, and as the whole is related to ends. This is a necessary condition for rational choice, but would not be sufficient as a condition for the highest form of freedom. It would not furnish an alternative in kind. For that we must have a moral nature. A moral nature involves obligation, but obligation is obligation to choose as between higher and lower ends. Whenever the alternative is presented of a choice between a higher and a lower end, a moral nature must affirm obligation to choose the higher, and the alternative in kind will present itself when the question is whether we will follow that impulse which the moral nature sanctions, or whether we will be governed by some stronger impulse or passion which the moral nature does not sanction. In such a case, if the man were to be governed by the impulse sanctioned by his conscience it would commonly be said that he was governed by his conscience. In a sense he is, but only indirectly. He is directly governed by some natural principle of action other than conscience, but calls upon conscience to decide which it shall be.

When a rational being is brought to the point of choice between two principles of action different in kind, he knows that he has power to choose in either direction, and cannot avoid feeling responsible for his choice.

It was by these powers, thus related and acting thus, that man was in the image of God ; and the first result, as stated in Genesis, of the possession by him of these powers, was that he should have *dominion*. Dominion — this is the first result mentioned in the Bible of man as fully constituted, and this we are now to consider. That the powers mentioned, and these only, would fit man for dominion is evident, because these, and these only, legitimately used, would give him wisdom and righteousness, which are the essential qualifications for dominion.

But the image of God was not all that was needed to fit man for dominion. He needed also to be in right relations with that over which he was to have dominion. This, also, was provided for. His creation in the image of God did not preclude his creation in the image of all that was below him. The Bible represents him as the last and highest of a series, and as such it was to be expected that he should be in harmony with that series. It is upon his relations to what is below him, and his harmony with that, that naturalists have chiefly fixed their attention, while theologians and moralists have chiefly fixed their attention on him as related to what was above him. The object of the one class has been and is to show the resemblances between man and the brutes, and thus to bring them as near as possible together, making, in fact, no essential difference between them. The object of the other class has been and is to show the differences between them, and thus to separate them as widely as possible. The truth will be found, and not only that, but the fitness of man for dominion, by looking candidly at both the resemblances and the differences.

Marvelous is the correspondence between man and nature; so marvelous that there is a broad basis for the doctrine of correspondencies as set forth by Swedenborg and his followers. This doctrine is true, and has been too much neglected by us. Man strikes his roots into nature. She is his mother; he is a part of her. Born into her uniformities and ongoings, he finds himself at home among them. There is not an aspect in which she shows herself in the changes of day and night and of the seasons, in repose and movement, in sublimity and beauty, with which he does not sympathize. These are for impression. Through these she is related to the emotions; but in her regular movements and uniform structures she furnishes ground for classification and appeals to thought. No arrangement can be conceived better fitted to awaken the emotions and to call out and train the intellect.

Nor, if we turn from unconscious nature to the animal creation, is the correspondence less striking. It is more so. It is this correspondence that has been specially studied of late, and has given plausibility to the theory that man was developed from the brute. This correspondence is seen not only in the sympathy there is between some animals and man and in the analogy of their faculties, but also in the extent to which the qualities of animals are ascribed to man.

This correspondence of man with what is below him, whether unconscious or sentient, is perhaps best seen in the history and structure of language. It is supposed that all words expressive of mental operations originally signified some analogous physical act or condition. When Christ says, "Walk in the light while ye have the light lest darkness come upon you," we have no thought of literal walking, or of literal light or darkness. When He called Herod a fox, or the scribes and Pharisees a generation of vipers, or said that salt was good, no one failed to comprehend Him.

We are not, then, to think of man as created arbitrarily, with no reference to what had gone before, but are to see in this intimate relationship one of those provisions by which he became fitted to exercise the prerogatives which belonged to him as made in the image of God. Evidently, the more perfectly man could reflect in his emotions the aspects of nature, and comprehend by his intellect her structures and movements, and embody in his language her significance, and the more fully he could take up into himself and so sympathize with the animal creation, the more perfectly would he be fitted to be the king and priest of this lower world. Without the image of God, the more any being in the form of man should be identified with nature the less would he be fitted to have dominion over it; with that image so revealed as to enable him to put nature under his feet, the more he should be identified with it the more would he be fitted to rule over it and to mediate as a priest between nature and God, offering up intelligent sacrifices of praise. Kingship and priesthood, — these are the two offices for which man is fitted by being in the image of God. His priesthood is not mentioned in Genesis, but is recognized throughout the Bible. He can recognize, and he only, the manifestation of the attributes of God in nature, and can give intelligent expression of adoration and praise in view of such manifestation; and this the more perfectly the more fully he understands nature and is in sympathy with it.

And here we find a beautiful analogy between the mode in which man was fitted to become the king and priest of nature and the mode in which Christ became fitted to be the king and priest of man. Christ became fitted to be our king and priest by assuming our nature, and the more fitted the more perfectly He partook of it, so as to be in all points like us, except sin, while yet He could be our king and priest only as He had also a nature higher than ours. In the same way, man could not have been fitted to be the king and priest of all below him, except by being a partaker of it all, while yet his kingship was not from that, but from the image of God superinduced upon that and united with it.

Let the naturalist, then, bring man into as close affinity with nature and with animals as he pleases; the closer the better, if it be but distinctly seen that he is capable of dominion and of priesthood. Give us these, or the possibility of these, in man, and we ask for no wider ground of separation between man and the brutes; for of dominion, in the proper sense of that word, dominion over itself, over nature, or over its fellows, no brute can know anything, nor can it know anything of an intelligent mediation between nature and God. Being destitute of rational and moral elements, the brute cannot have the first dawning of either of these ideas. The idea of dominion implies a comprehension and choice of ends, and a direction of ourselves or others towards the ends which we choose. It supposes a double nature in man, and ends higher and lower. It supposes freedom, for if man were under the same law of necessity as nature and the brutes, any conception of dominion would be impossible.

This is a point which I wish to emphasize, because it shows that the Scriptural idea of man is that of a free being lifted above those fixed laws of necessity by which nature and the animals are governed, and not only lifted above them, but able, by a varying adjustment among themselves of unvarying laws, to exercise dominion. This he can do only as he is free. It is self-evident that no being, under the law of necessity, can have dominion. It is in this idea of freedom, — liberty of choice with an alternative in kind by a being who comprehends ends, and in the dominion through intelligence and will consequent upon that, — that we find the culmination of our idea of man as possessed of natural endowments, and, indeed, the culmination of our idea of God himself. This liberty or freedom is not spontaneity. It is not automatic or unconscious obedience to law. Nor is it lawlessness. A being having liberty is still under law. He is morally bound to choose according to the law of his being, but is not necessitated to choose thus. In choosing thus, he is both virtuous and wise, and in carrying out his choices he finds, scope according to his capacity, for intelligence and will in each of the spheres in which dominion can be exercised.

These spheres are three. The first he finds in himself. According to what has been said he has in himself nature and all the animals, and his dominion must begin by a thorough rule over these as a part of himself. Hence, because he has the animals in himself, among most primitive people men have been named from animals, and some of those names are still retained. Thus, we have among us Lions spelt with a y, and Foxes, and Wolfs, and Lambs, and Bulls, and Colts, and Hoggs, and Oysters. The birds are not so well represented, but we have Hawks and Doves, Robins, Wrens, and Martins. But other animals are in man besides those whose names are attached to them. Our Saviour called men serpents and vipers; an apostle said: "Beware of dogs;" and if we may believe men as they sometimes speak of each other, they *are* dogs, and puppies, and asses, and even skunks. Clearly, then, the first thing requisite is for a man, not to eradicate, but to rule over all that is in him that is natural and animal. He who does not exercise full dominion here is unfitted for any other.

The second sphere of man's dominion is over nature and the animals as he finds them outside of himself. In this sphere his dominion is evidently most limited and imperfect compared with what it would have been if he had not lost dominion over himself. What that would have been, I suppose we see in Christ, and in his dominion over nature. He was a man in perfect sympathy with God, and for such a man, what we now call miraculous power, would, I suppose, be a matter of course.

The third sphere of man's dominion is, that over his fellow-men, as they are placed under him through the natural relations of parent and child, and of civil government. In this sphere, too, there has been great imperfection and disorder, but great as these have been, they have sprung wholly from the original failure of man to retain dominion over himself.

Thus it is that through this idea of dominion, as growing out of the image of God, we are able to find the place of man, and to see how it is that he is connected, both with that which is below him, and with that which is above him. Most intimately is he connected with all that is below him. It is a part of his nature. From all that is below him he is at the same time most widely separated. The connection is through the law of the conditioning and the conditioned, since he is conditioned on all that is below him. The separation is through the addition from without and from above, of that which is capable of dominion. I say from without and from above, because it is impossible that freedom should be developed from necessity, or that a capacity for dominion should be developed out of that over which the dominion is to be exercised.

Thus do we harmonize different views by supposing that the creation was built and not developed; that the advancing movement was not by development from within, through the agency of an unconscious power, but by additions from without and from above, through the agency of an intelligent builder. This view gives to the naturalist in the controversy that is now going on all the time that he needs, and also the affinity between man and the lower animals; and it gives to the spiritualist all that he claims in a controlling and wise agency from without.

After the image of God, and dominion from that, the next feature of the Scriptural idea of man is that our one common humanity was created male and female. "And God said, Let us make man in our image, after our likeness, and let *them* have dominion." "So God created man in his own image, in the image of God created He him, male and female created He them." In both these passages the word "them" is evidently put in apposition with the word "man," so that here, as elsewhere, the word man, used generically, includes woman. The creation of *a* man without a woman would not have been the creation of man.

This feature of the Scriptural idea is among the most marvelous connected with the race, and more than upon anything else that is earthly, does the well-being of the race depend upon the right apprehension and adjustment of the relation constituted by it. What we need to know is the Scriptural, that is, the divine idea of this relation, and of the social arrangements and duties that should result from it. If man would use his limbs or faculties aright he must use them for the ends designed by God, and in a manner adapted to secure those ends; and if a social state was to be constituted, and the race perpetuated, and civil society and governments established through the sexual relation, we should expect that this would be done with success only as men should recognize and conform to the divine idea. Here, as everywhere, it is the business of man to find the divine idea, and work according to that. "For see, said He, that thou make all things according to the pattern showed to thee in the mount."

This is of the more consequence, because organizations on a false basis perpetuate themselves with a downward tendency, and fall into complications and corruptions from which there has hitherto been no escape except through convulsion and blood. The material interests of men become dependent on such organizations, children grow up in them, their associations become conformed to them, and thus, however iniquitous and disastrous, they may not only come to have the sanction of established usage, but may even be held sacred. When this is the case, if individuals are to be reached and elevated, it must be at a great disadvantage; and if a reformer arise with a clear apprehension of the divine ideal, and would seek to bring society and its usages into conformity with that, he must do it at the peril of his reputation, and often of his life. It is in this way that society falls into what were called in the time of the anti-slavery agitation organic sins; and the result of these, when they once become fairly imbedded in society, generally is that they go on till the evil becomes so great that, as was said by Livy of the evils of his day among the Romans, they can be neither cured nor endured.

And here I may be permitted to say that perhaps we do not sufficiently appreciate the advantage our fathers had in beginning anew on this continent, where they were compelled to look to the future rather than to the past, where they were invited to form new ideals, and where intelligence and the spirit of freedom might have scope to cast new moulds into which society should be run. And sure I am, that we are not sufficiently aware of the danger we are in of having the work of our fathers, in their apprehension of higher ideals, and in the formation of better moulds, overflowed and swamped by a steady and unmodified current of emigration.

But, as the relation of the sexes is at the foundation of the family, and so of all other institutions, it is especially desirable that our conception of the divine idea concerning that should be correct.

The first characteristic to be noticed is the peculiar unity of which I have already spoken, by which man and woman are equally constituents and factors of a common humanity. Each is essential and equally essential, both to the full idea of the race, and to its perpetuity. The conception of the race is not completed by masculine qualities, either physical or mental. The strength and executive ability of man are no more needed for a complete idea of humanity than the beauty and tenderness of woman. Each was, therefore, created with such reference to the other as to constitute a unity in one race; each was equally blessed of God, and to each equally was dominion given. "So God created *man* in his own image, in the image of God created He him; male and female created He them. And God blessed them; and God said unto them, Be fruitful and multiply, and replenish the earth and subdue it; and have dominion over the fish of the sea, and over the fowl of the air, and over every living thing." So perfectly were the first man and woman regarded by God as constituting a unity of race, that He gave them but one name. "The name given by Adam to the woman was Eve, "because she was the mother of all living," but the name given her by God, and the only name, was Adam. Thus, we read, "In the day that God created man, in the likeness of God made He him. Male and female created He them, and called *their* name *Adam* in the day when they were created." Not in virtue of being married to Adam, but of being created as Adam was, and in the unity of a common nature, did Eve share with him a common name.

But this unity in diversity of beings of the same race was only preparatory to the higher union of man and woman in marriage. In this we have the second and great characteristic of the Scriptural idea of man as a race. It comprises all that is involved in marriage, and in the perpetuation of the race through the union of one man with one woman. That the union of one man with one woman in a true marriage, through such mutual admiration and affection that the coolest reason would sanction the most ardent feeling, would lay the best foundation for the happiness of the two sexes, and would furnish the best condition for continuing, and educating, and elevating the race, there can be no question. This all history shows. It would exclude, on the one hand, licentiousness in its irregular forms, together with concubinage and polygamy, and on the other hand celibacy inculcated as a system, and claiming peculiar sanctity. But this is precisely the provision for the happiness of the race involved in the Scriptural idea of man. Let us look at this.

That the Scriptures require in marriage the union of one man with one woman it would be superfluous to show, but it may be well to see how this is provided for, and insisted on. ⌜It was provided for in the first instance by the creation of but a single woman.⌝ This is a strong point. "And did not He," says the prophet Malachi, "make one?" "Yet had He the residue of the Spirit." He might have made any number. "And wherefore one? That He might seek a godly seed." On this point our Saviour insisted repeatedly in opposition to the permission of Moses, and to the spirit and practice of the time, insomuch that his disciples were astonished, and were led to question whether marriage would be desirable under such restrictions; and He made the basis of his teaching this original constitution by God. It is wonderful how decided and authoritative He was. At that time, and on that subject, only a divine teacher could have been so. "And the Pharisees came to Him and asked Him, Is it lawful for a man to put away his wife? tempting Him. And He answered and said unto them, What did Moses command you? And they said, Moses suffered to write a bill of divorcement, and to put her away. And Jesus answered and said unto them, For the hardness of your heart he wrote you this precept. But from the beginning of the creation God made them male and female. For this cause shall a man leave his father and mother and cleave to his wife; and they twain shall be one flesh; so then they are no more twain, but one flesh. What, therefore, God hath joined together let not man put asunder." Than these, perhaps the same number of words were never uttered that have affected the social condition of the world more widely, or more beneficially. To this teaching of Christ the Apostles fully conformed.

But the Scriptural idea of marriage was spoken of not only as the idea of one man with one woman, but as a union based on affection. How is that indicated? It is indicated, first, by the mode in which the woman was created. She was not taken from the common earth, but from a part of man. "Not," as Matthew Henry says, "out of his head to top him, nor out of his feet to be trampled on by him; but out of his side to be equal with him, under his arm to be protected, and near his heart to be beloved." This Adam understood, for he said when she was brought to him, "This is now bone of my bones, and flesh of my flesh." No words more expressive of the closest union, and of the strongest affection, could have been used. "Bone of my bones, and flesh of my flesh." And it is in harmony with this when that is immediately added, which is quoted and sanctioned by our Saviour, "Therefore shall a man leave his father and his mother, and shall cleave unto his wife; and they shall be one flesh." A paramount affection would be the only one consonant with a union so intimate. In accordance with this is the teaching of Paul, who says, "So ought men to love their wives as their own bodies. He that loveth his wife loveth himself."

What then, for we are now prepared to see that, is the whole Scriptural idea of man regarded as male and female? It is first the idea of a unity of race, and then of a unity in the marriage of one man with one woman which is to be for life, and is to be based on a paramount affection. This was Adam's idea, — "bone of my bones, and flesh of my flesh," — and it has not been improved upon since. Here was the most delicate and complex relation of all time, one involving all human interests, and yet no statesman or philosopher has been able to improve upon the ideal of it that Adam had and expressed when God first brought his wife to him. Men have invented spinning jennies and telegraphs, and have made progress in many things, but in a right apprehension of the underlying relation of society they have not gone beyond Adam. He struck the key-note of social harmony for all time.

In speaking of man and woman, as a unity, we are to distinguish between unity and a unit, and also between that and union. A unit has no parts. A unity is a whole made up of parts that are complemental of each other. Union may exist where there is no whole and no unity, as between men who unite for a common object. The human body is a unity, and it is so because it is a whole that is complete through the right position and ministration of every part. Marriage is a union, but the peculiarity of it is that it is a union between those who are capable of becoming a unity, and are not only capable of it, but are so preconformed to it in their whole being that their full development and highest life cannot be reached without it. This is the general rule, though there are doubtless individual exceptions. In this view of it the problem in every marriage will be to form a union that will constitute a perfect unity. This implies that neither the man nor the woman, regarded as an individual, is a whole, and that there is in each that which is complemental of the other. Hence the most perfect unity will require, not similarity, nor opposition, but correspondence, and the whole which each will equally constitute, and in which both will find their common sphere, for really it is but one, is the family and the home.

But if the family and the home be a common sphere, on what principle are its duties and responsibilities to be allotted? Where the Scriptural law of marriage has been observed, this has always regulated itself in accordance with the indications of the male and female constitution, and with those sentiments of homage and devotion which a true man will always feel towards a true woman, and which, next to religion, have done more than anything else to purify and elevate the race. Under these conditions, the husband has always provided for his own, with the aid of the wife, and the wife has guided the house with the aid of her husband.

The diversity in unity of which I have spoken as much requires that there should be a head of the family as that there should be a head of the body; and on this point the teaching of the Scriptures is unequivocal. They make the man the head of the family. This is in accordance with the analogy of nature below man, and so with the responsibilities which belong to him from his constitution. Uniformly among animals the male is the leader and protector. It is not because a flock of wild geese are *geese* that they are always led by a gander; it is because it is in accordance with a law of the animal creation. But while the Scriptures make man the head of the family, they make him its head as Christ is the head of the church. The headship is one of love and protection. Nor does it follow that the superiority implied in headship is not counterbalanced by other forms of superiority, so that equality, on the whole, is preserved. If we use the words head and heart, with reference to the individual, either literally or metaphorically, who can say which is superior? They are mutually dependent, and each is admirable and best in its place.

The family thus constituted, with its head for direction and its heart for love, suffices to itself. It constitutes a peculiar society, into which children are born, of which they become a part not by their own choice but by the ordinance of God, and on which they so depend that no man comes into life as an isolated individual. The theory which regards society as originally founded by equals unrelated and independent, and as deriving its obligations and authority from a compact between them, has no foundation in fact. Man is, and with the exception of the first pair, who were created into it, always has been, born into the family. This may and ought to be a society that shall furnish adequate conditions for the well-being of man, both here and hereafter.

It must have done so to Adam and Eve for many years. They did not begin their married life by boarding, and there was no club-house or bar-room to which Adam could go. The family constituted the one sphere of social life, for the perfection and results of which the presence and efforts of the husband and wife were equally necessary, for which they were equally responsible, and into which the children would naturally and imperceptibly grow, as sharing its pleasures and assuming its duties and responsibilities. In doing this they would have the best advantages possible for fitting them for their future positions as heads of families, and for being trained to the self-denials and restraints required by civil society, when that should become necessary.

The family is the first society established by God. It is especially legislated for in the ten commandments. It is the seed-plot of civil society. It not only gives it its materials, but determines their character. Let the father and the mother both give their best efforts to the family, and the home and civil society will readily adjust itself in its form to the demand of the times, and will be easily administered. I desire, therefore, to magnify the family as a sphere complete in itself, and admitting of no contrast with any other that would imply that the husband and the wife are not equally responsible for the results. I still hold, and strongly, that the family is the unit of civil society, and that free governments for such society must be representative; but whether its representatives shall be men only, or both men and women, so that they shall be equal factors in political life, is to be decided, not by inquiring whether the family is properly and fully the sphere of man, but whether government, as the agent of civil society, is properly, and should be made fully, the sphere of woman.

I dwell on this subject because it is one of present interest, and because the efforts at reform do not seem to trend towards the Scriptural idea, but the reverse. The Scriptural idea is that every man is to have his own wife and every woman her own husband, who is to love her with a paramount affection as bone of his bones and flesh of his flesh. So was it with Adam and Eve. This was one element of the Paradisaical state, and the true reform would be in or towards the realization of this. A true reform would intensify the unity there is in marriage, it would magnify the family, and it would insist more upon duties than upon rights. But what now calls itself reform tends towards separation rather than unity. It seeks, not so much interdependence, as individual independence, especially the independence of woman, and it insists more upon rights than upon duties. Where duties are recognized and rightly met, there can be no need of contending about rights; and in relations where affection and courtesy ought to rule that cannot be the happiest condition in which rights are gained and held only as they are contended for.

That there are evils demanding a remedy there can be no question. These have arisen partly from laws that have ignored the rights of women when those rights needed legal protection; they have arisen more from a want of affection and of right principle that would have prevented any question about rights, and especially have they arisen from a violation of other laws of God that have no direct relation to marriage. There is a solidarity in the laws of God by which the breaking of one brings derangement into the whole moral life and into all social relations. It is by war, and by emigration in a way that puts the desires, especially the desire of property, as an element of happiness above the affections, that a state of things has come about, both in this country and in Europe, that seems to justify the efforts of professional agitators ; for which, as exceptional, perhaps special modifications should be made, but for which no adequate remedy is possible till society shall obey the laws of God in other respects.

For the marriage of one man with one woman, according to the pattern set in Eden, God made provision by an excess in the number of male children sufficient to cover the loss from the greater exposures incident to the life of man, — just that and no more. When, then, men are slain in war by the half million, as they were in the wars of Napoleon I., or in the Franco-Prussian war, or in our own civil war, or when they are slain in the prime of their life, as they have been in all wars, it becomes impossible that every woman should have her own husband, and a home which she can make happy. It is to be said, also, that standing armies and camp and garrison life involve conditions that render marriage and the proper relations of the family impossible, and, if they do not necessitate, yet insure those relations of the sexes that are wholly incompatible with the Scriptural idea. ⌐In this respect England has been peculiarly unfortunate; for, in addition to her wars and standing armies, she has had distant colonies that have drained away her young men, so that the excess of women in her population is very great. ⌐And so chronic and hopeless has this become that I recently saw it stated that there is growing up there a class of women who repudiate marriage, and in whom the instinct towards it seems to have been lost.⌐ So, also, from the combined influence of the late war and of emigration, is it in a measure in New England. The social elements are not rightly adjusted.⌐

Here there is an evil and a wrong, but it is one which no amount of agitation or legislation can remove. Like all chronic evils, it can be removed only by time and by a return to those principles through a violation of which the evil has come. Meantime, if there is to be a large number of women unmarried, and not set in families as God intended they should be, so that they are to come into the same relations to men that men do to each other, then as far and as fast as they come into the same relations and share the same responsibilities, they should have the same rights, and especially should everything possible be done to open to them all those lines of employment upon which they are fitted to enter and through which they may gain an honorable independence.

⌐But while there may thus be palliations, while the agitation itself is to many a palliation, like taking a remedy that does no good except from the feeling that something is being done, let not men or women suppose that the deep wants of our nature can be thus met, or that the true remedy lies in this direction. No, it lies in the direction of the Scriptural idea of the marriage of one man with one woman, who shall be "bone of his bones and flesh of his flesh."

VI.

MAN IN HIS PRESENT STATE. — "THE MAN CHRIST JESUS."

HITHERTO we have considered man, as the Scriptures represent him to have been in his original state. What do they say of him in his present state?

In his present state they represent him as both sinful and corrupt. He still retains the image of God in his natural attributes so far that God is his Father and yearns over him, but he has lost the moral image of God, and no language can be stronger than that of the Scriptures to express the guilt and danger of his condition. "They are all under sin." "There is none righteous; no, not one." "They are all gone out of the way, they are together become unprofitable; there is none that doeth good, no, not one." "They say unto God, Depart from us, we desire not a knowledge of thy ways." "There is no fear of God before their eyes." "Corrupt are they, and have done abominable wickedness." These representations are confirmed by the history of the race. That history is largely, and, when men have been left to themselves, chiefly, one of war, of slavery, of cruelty, of lust, of fraud, of gain by ministering to degrading appetites, of hypocrisy, of superstition, of perversion of the material gifts of God, and especially of persecution, and of fiendish cruelty in the very name of the religion of peace and good will. ⌈No contrast can be greater than that between the actual history of this world and what that history might have been, and would have been if man had obeyed the physical laws of his constitution and the moral laws of God.⌋

I have said that the Scriptures represent man as both guilty and corrupt. Between guilt and corruption a distinction may be made if we refer guilt to the action of the will or spiritual powers, and corruption to the action of those involuntary powers of the mind which are analogous to the involuntary powers of the body. What it is that originally sets in motion that involuntary current of the mind which the will certainly did not originate, and which it cannot stop, no one can tell. Perhaps no one can tell what determines the particular thoughts and feelings that it presents; but it is conceivable that it might present only what would be acceptable to an enlightened reason and a pure conscience; and, also, that it might present thoughts and feelings wholly the reverse. ⌈We all know with what force and persistency thoughts of evil and temptations will sometimes come to us.⌋ What is possible in this direction may be seen in those cases of madness in which the voluntary power wholly loses its control, and the utterances express whatever is presented by the involuntary power. When this is the case those utterances are sometimes nothing but a continuous stream of shameless indecencies and appalling blasphemies. This is utter corruption, and there may be corruption analogous to this to almost any degree while the personal power retains its control. Sin is the admission and acceptance by the person of anything that is opposed to reason and conscience, and the law of God. Temptation does not imply either sin or corruption. The temptation may come from without. Nor would I say that all temptation through our own nature implies corruption, but only that which comes after sin. The voluntary and involuntary powers act and react upon each other, and when once the man has sinned the quality of the involuntary movements of the mind becomes changed, they become corrupt.

And here, in the way that sin and corruption come into the spiritual realm, we find one of those analogies to what takes place in the lower forms of being that show the unity of the system throughout. All disintegration and corruption of matter is from the domination of a lower over a higher force or law. The body begins to return to its original elements as the lower chemical and physical forces begin to gain ascendency over the higher force of life. In the same way all sin and corruption in man is from his yielding to a lower law or principle of action in opposition to the demands of one that is higher.

Seeing thus what it is to be sinful, and what to be corrupt, we say that the Scriptures represent man as both sinful and corrupt. They represent the race as universally yielding to a lower principle of action rather than to that love of God with all the heart, and of the neighbor as himself, by which they say he ought to be governed, and which can be shown by a fair analysis to be the highest law of his being. Of the two generic kinds of character heretofore spoken of, they represent man as universally forming that one which makes supreme some impulsive principle of action, or self-love, rather than one that recognizes and accepts and seeks to maintain the supremacy of that law of God which commands us to love, and that authority of conscience over the will by which the command is enforced. The sin of Adam was, that he rejected God as a guide and portion, and chose himself as a guide and the world as a portion; and this, account for it as we may, his descendants uniformly do. They do not submit themselves to God. They do not love Him supremely, and in thus choosing some principle of action, lower than the highest, they take an attitude which would infallibly lead them, when carried consistently to its results, to crucify Christ and to dethrone God himself. If God will provide for them, and let them have their own way, they will be conscious of no opposition to Him; but if He deal with them in a way to show that He has a controversy with them an opposition will be awakened, and one that must continue till the question of authority shall be settled.

And here it may be remarked, that we find in this opposition of man to God, and in his consequent degradation, an evidence of his high origin scarcely less conclusive than in that original image of God in which he was created. In that prerogative of man, by which he can either accept or reject the law of his being, he differs wholly from any mere animal. No animal can approximate anything of the kind. It lies in a sphere and region of which it knows nothing. We have here, indeed, a fundamental, perhaps the most fundamental difference, between man and the brute. By accepting the law of his being man is capable of rising to a height of knowledge, of goodness, of dominion, which show *that* in him which must be wholly different in its origin from anything in the brute. Also, by rebelling against God and rejecting the law of his being, he is capable of sinking to a degradation so far below the brute, as to show equally that they could not have had a common origin. No brute is any more capable of rebelling against God than of serving Him, is no more capable of sinking below the level of its own nature than of rising to the level of the nature of man. No brute can be either a fool or a fiend. The Scriptural idea of man then, in his present state, is that of a being capable of an indefinite progress, either upward or downward, and of choosing which it shall be.

We have now considered the Scriptural idea of man as created; as in the image of God in knowledge; in feeling; in his moral nature; and in dominion. We have also considered the Scriptural idea of man as he is in his present state. But all the capabilities of man and his possible relations, as the Scriptures represent them, can be known by us only as we consider "*The Man Christ Jesus.*"

And here the first thing to be noticed is, the impossibility that Jesus Christ, as He stands before us in the Gospels, should have been the product of his age. Any supposition that He could have been developed, or evolved from anything in that, or, indeed, in any age, can arise only from a failure to appreciate the elevation, the isolation, and entire originality of his character and work. He was wholly separated from his age in his *object* in the *standard of greatness* He established, and in his *method*.

His *object* was a change of character in men that should fit them for citizenship in a kingdom of righteousness, over which He was to reign after His death and resurrection. It is spoken of by the Apostle Peter, as "the everlasting kingdom of our Lord and Saviour Jesus Christ." Except incidentally and indirectly, that kingdom had nothing to do with the interests of this world, and yet it had everything to do with them, since the character needed for citizenship in the future kingdom is just the character, and the only character, that can give peace, and prosperity, and a permanently progressive civilization here. This kingdom He made in no respect exclusive. He did not base it at all, as Jewish bigotry would have prompted, on race or nationality, but solely on character; and He made citizenship in it equally free to all the world. Think, then, what it was for a young man, a Jew, one of a conquered people, without learning, or wealth, or power, despised as a Jew by other nations, and rejected by his own, to assert persistently that He was a king, a king of a kingdom not of this world, to assert it when a prisoner, bound and sentenced to death, and to abate no whit of his claim under the mockery of a purple robe, and of a reed for a sceptre, and of a crown of thorns! Was this madness? Was it even extravagance? Let that kingdom of love, of which Napoleon spoke, and over which Christ now reigns, answer. Let the facts that the conception is the grandest possible, and that we find in it the only satisfactory solution of the problem of this world, answer. And was He who had such an object, and who bore Himself in a manner corresponding with it, and over against whose life and death such results and such possibilities stand, the product of such an age as that? Of any age?

Again, that the Man Christ Jesus could not have been the product of his age, is clear from the standard of greatness which He established in that kingdom of which I have just spoken. This was something till then wholly unheard of, and unthought of. It was not physical prowess, or mental superiority, or wealth, or power, or even culture. It was *self-sacrificing love*, — service from that. "Whosoever will be great among you, let him be your minister; and whosoever will be chief among you, let him be your servant. Even as the Son of man came, not to be ministered unto, but to minister, and to give his life a ransom for many." In simply setting up this standard, and giving this example, He opened a career of greatness, and of the noblest ambition, to the humblest and most obscure of the race. This was something, the reach and significance of which has been even as yet but little appreciated. Looked at from the standard of the world, even now, what hope is there of greatness, of distinction of any kind for a poor sewing woman, or for a servant girl, or for him who, by his daily toil, earns his daily bread? None, none. But in the kingdom of Christ all this may be reversed. There, there are first that shall be last, and last that shall be first. O, thou poor widow making thy way towards the place where gifts are put into the treasury, with thy two mites that are all thy living carefully done up, the passing scribe does not notice thee as these mites fall in, nor the Pharisee with his phylacteries, nor the priest in his robes; but there is One, clothed in a seamless coat, who does, and who shall make thee the standard of greatness in giving for all time. O, thou dweller in some poor cottage who hast given a cup of cold water to a disciple in the name of a disciple, the world has not known thee, it never will; but there is One who knows thee, and makes thee the example of hospitality in his kingdom. Nor is there any preference shown to the poor. The rich woman — she must have been relatively rich — who poured the box of precious ointment on the head of the Saviour shall have her work spoken of wherever this gospel is preached. This standard is clearly the true one for the race, because it is the only one within the reach of all. This *is* within the reach of all, and no one can estimate its uplifting power, or the changed relations of the race if it could but be fully realized and accepted. Let it but be freely understood, that the welcome, "Well done, thou good and faithful servant, enter thou into the joy of thy Lord," may await the poorest and the humblest, no less than the most distinguished, and there would be a cheer, and a warmth, and a comfort in the heart of the neglected and despised that nothing else could give. My friends, Christendom is not Christian yet. Far from it. It will not be till Christ's standard of greatness is fully accepted. What then, let me ask you, was there in that age of grasping selfishness, of unscrupulous ambition, of Jewish animosity smothered, and of Roman contempt openly avowed, what had there been in any age to suggest such a standard of greatness, or such an opening to the race of a sphere of activity suited to all, and that would be sure, if accepted, ultimately to lift all to the highest point attainable by humanity? The contrast is great, almost too great for belief; and yet think what it is for a poor, neglected, dying man, who has been "patient in well-doing," — that is the condition, — to have whispered into his ear the words: "glory, honor, immortality, eternal life;" but these are the words that Christ whispers into the ear of such. Mock at it if you will, and some will mock at it, but herein is an infinite love, and an infinite hope.

Again, that Christ was not the product of his age is clear from his method. His method was that which the hero worshipers of this later day have seen to be the true one. Man was not made to be governed by abstract speculations or systems. The discussions of the Academy, the speculations of philosophers have had little influence over the masses, except as they have been understood to open the door of license. No instance can be given of a people who have been elevated in that way. Men need a leader, an example, a *person* to whom they can look as a centre of attraction. This has been seen, and so there has been an outcry for *the* man, the coming *man*. But the man does not come. He never will. He *has* come, and they reject him; and every hero that comes now shrivels on inspection. No system ever stirred the hearts of men, or awakened such enthusiasm as did the person of Napoleon. But, even if he had been the great man he was supposed to be, his person was a possible centre of attraction only to Frenchmen. So has it been with nations and with clans. Their enthusiasm for the person who most fully embodied their special ideas has been intense, and they have been weak without it. Hear Scott when Clan Alpine was attacked, while Roderick Dhu was wounded and a prisoner:—

> "Oh, where was Roderick then?
> One blast upon *his* bugle horn
> Were worth a thousand men."

When great deeds are to be done, the nation, the clan, need a person as the leader and centre of attraction, and so do the race. As such a leader and centre Christ has come. He claims to be such a centre. The method of his kingdom is *the union to himself of his subjects by a paramount love*. To this even the most sacred affections were to be subordinated. "If any man come to me and hate not his father, and mother, and wife, and children, and brethren, and sisters, yea, and his own life also, he cannot be my disciple." "And I, if I be lifted up, will draw *all men* unto me." Here was his method. He was, Himself, in his own person, by the manifestation of his love on the cross, to be the centre of attraction and of union for the race. But what a conception! How impossible that a young man, a Jew, with not "where to lay his head," should have conceived that by suffering as a malefactor the most ignominious and painful death then known, He should become the centre of attraction to the race! And yet, to-day, there is no other being who has ever lived on the earth towards whom so many hearts are drawn. The necessity of such a centre is, as I have said, felt, but wealth, and fashion, and literature, and culture reject Christ. He is to them "a root out of dry ground." They form separate centres and coteries, with common admiration of some one, and mutual admiration of each other, but the masses do not know them. Knowing nothing of sin or redemption, the deep wants of humanity are not reached, and they pass. They agree in but one thing, and that is, to either ignore or restrict the influence of Christ. It is now nearly forty years since the first volume of Emerson's Essays was published. That volume I bought and read with pleasure. The second volume I also bought when that appeared, but before reading it much, if at all, I happened to open to this passage: "Jesus would absorb the race; but Tom Paine, or the coarsest blasphemer, helps humanity by resisting this exuberance of power."[1] I immediately closed the book, and did

[1] *Essays*, Second Series, p. 263.

not open it again till after the death of Emerson. It seemed to me so dreadful that "the coarsest blasphemer" should be welcomed as a benefactor of the race if he could only limit the influence of Him who was, and is, to me, the Redeemer of the race, the second Adam, *the man*, and whose influence was, for me, the hope of the race. I believe that if this world is ever to be ruled in righteousness the sceptre of power will be held, virtually, if not literally, by the hand that bears the "print of the nails." I believe that He who was once crowned with thorns shall yet be crowned with many crowns. I believe, too, that he who does the most, in whatever form, whether of art, or culture, or what may call itself religion, to obstruct and limit the influence of Jesus, is he who does the most to obstruct the progress of the race.

Looking, then, at these three particulars only, — the object of Jesus, his standard of greatness, and his method, — I think we must see that such a phenomenon as Christ must baffle utterly all theories of gradualism or of outgrowth from his age, and that we shall assent to the account of Him given by Himself, "I am from above."

Having shown that the man Christ Jesus was not the product of his age, my next remark is that He was so man that every man becomes more a man as he becomes more like Him, and that every woman becomes more a woman as she becomes more like Him. This is presupposed by his method. If, by becoming a Christian, a man does not become more truly man according to God's conception of manhood and as

He would have him to be, and if, in becoming a Christian, a woman does not come to be more fully woman according to God's conception of womanhood and as He would have her to be, then Christianity is a failure. This must be so, for Christ being, according to his method, *the* man, the centre of attraction to the race, that law of moral assimilation must hold by which moral beings are changed into the image of that which they contemplate with pleasure; and if there were not that in Christ which would thus bring to its full perfection the proper nature of each, there would be an arrest of progress, and failure. Accordingly, as has often been remarked, there was in Christ a combination of masculine and feminine qualities and traits such as has been found in no one else. He had the stronger traits, the higher wisdom, the severer virtues of man, in perfect combination with the more instinctive wisdom, the tenderness, and refinement of woman. At the same time, He was free, both in his character and in his teaching, from anything local or sectional or national, so that He was the only man who has ever lived who could thus become a centre of attraction to the race. All may be equally attracted to Him, and through Him to each other, so that in Him there shall be "neither Jew nor Greek, neither bond nor free, neither male nor female," but all shall be "one in Christ Jesus." Any other individual of the race, so free from peculiarities of nation and of race that he could become equally a centre of attraction to all, it would be as difficult to find as one free from sin. But the man Christ Jesus claims to be such a person. He claims it not only by demanding paramount affection, but also by saying He will draw all men unto Him, and thus making it the method of His kingdom.

It is pleasing to know that, in our day, the Person of Christ, which He himself thus made central, is being recognized more and more among his followers as their true centre, instead of creeds and forms of church organization.

This claim that Christ is the centre for the race, and thus the true standard of manhood, needs to be more fully substantiated, and I proceed to do that, first, in one particular in which He could not be our example, and then in some particulars in which He could be and is.

The first particular is the sinlessness of "the man Christ Jesus."

In the apprehension of some, a sinless man would hardly be a man. But sin is the transgression by a man of the law of his being, and plainly, the nearer a man comes to obedience to the law of his being, the nearer does he come to a full manhood. The Bible account of the first man is, that he was originally, and for a time, sinless. "That Christ made this claim of sinlessness, and that his disciples made it for Him, there can be no doubt. They made it impliedly and they made it expressly. Christ said, "Which of you convinceth me of sin?"—that He did always those things that pleased the Father—that He was one with the Father. Peter says expressly that He did no sin, that He was the holy one and the just; and Paul says that He was "holy, harmless, undefiled, and separate from sinners." This claim can be accounted for only on the ground of a divine insight. It was the most extraordinary ever made, the most difficult to be sustained, wholly original, out of the line of ordinary thought, and in every human point of view superfluous. In carrying out its plans, what does the world care about sin? How, then, came this element to enter? — to enter as it did, not obtrusively, being scarcely affirmed, but pervasively, being everywhere assumed, as the being of God is in the Bible? How came the four Evangelists to be so accordant in this? In not one of them do we find that He repents, or asks forgiveness, or makes an apology, or expresses regret for anything He said or did, or faltered in any purpose. The reason is, that the claim and the fact on which it was based were essential to the system. If Christ was not sinless, the whole system would collapse. "There is," says the apostle, "one God and one Mediator between God and man, — the man Christ Jesus." But if He had been a sinner, He could not have been thus a Mediator. He would have needed one for Himself. Nor could He have been the Redeemer. Only the sinless one can redeem from sin. Nor, if He had Himself transgressed the law, could He be the final Judge of the race. But the point here is, that unless the man Christ Jesus had been sinless, He could not have been so *the* man that all human beings would approximate the perfection of their humanity in approximating Him.

As sinless, Christ cannot be our example, for we have all sinned; but He can be our standard. We now pass to some particulars in which He is fully our example. In speaking, however, of Christ as our example, it is obvious that He can be so only as He has a perfect humanity, and in those relations into which we may come. With what He was on the Godward side we have nothing here to do. It is also to be noticed that He cannot be our example in details, but only in his character, — only as He adopted certain great principles and manifested certain tempers which we may also adopt and manifest.

And the first particular we notice is his full acknowledgment of the fatherhood of God and his perfect submission to Him. It has been said that if Christ had done nothing else than to teach men to say "Our Father," He would have conferred on mankind more benefit than all the philosophers. And this we may well believe if we look at those conceptions of God which men have had that have led to such multitudes of human sacrifices and to such degrading rites. To substitute for such conceptions and for such rites the conception of God as a Father, and pure rites of worship, especially as connected with his providential care as taught by Christ, thus displacing terror and devil-worship by reverence and love, would indeed be doing more for the world than philosophy has ever done. Of the recognition of this fatherhood of God by Christ when He was twelve years old, we have an account, and in the whole account given we have such a recognition of it as to make his example perfect for us. He often retired for prayer; on all solemn occasions He looked up to God, and in the Garden and on the cross his submission to his Heavenly Father was put to the severest possible test. Here his example was perfect. We need just such a Heavenly Father, and just such submission and trust.

A second point to be noticed is the subordination by the man Christ Jesus of this world to another. The future and spiritual world were as real to Him as this, and He estimated them according to their relative importance. He was no cynic; He did not despise this world or its good things. He came eating and drinking. But he permitted no interest of this world to come between Him and what He owed to another. He assumed that other: never spoke of it as a matter of doubt. The mansions in his Father's house were spoken of in the same way as mansions here. He therefore made just the provision needed by Him for his wants in his peculiar position in this world, and no more. He owned no property. That would not have become Him; but He had provision suited to the wants of one who went about doing good. Here, then, we have an example greatly needed in its principle, but not generally applicable in its form. It is fit that men should own property and have where to lay their heads, but the world absorbs them. They idolize it. Their views and wishes and plans are limited by the horizon of time. As a rule, they do not seek first the kingdom of God and his righteousness. They do not lay up treasures in heaven. They are anxious about what they shall eat and drink and wear, or they throng the circles of gayety and fashion and pleasure, reckless of the future. Here, then, we have the greatest possible need of the application of the principle of our Saviour's example.

Once more. The man Christ Jesus set us a perfect example in choosing as supreme the highest possible principle of action. That that principle was *love* does not need to be shown at length. It was love in God that sent Him, and love in Him that brought Him. "Greater love hath no man than this, that a man lay down his life for his friend." "He loved us and gave Himself for us." "Who hath loved us and washed us from our sins in his own blood." In speaking of this love, the Apostle Paul falls into one of those paradoxes in which he abounds. "That Christ," he says, "may dwell in your hearts by faith, that ye, being rooted and grounded in love, may be able to comprehend, with all saints, what is the breadth and length and depth and height, and to know the love of Christ which passeth knowledge, that ye may be filled with all the fullness of God." This love, the highest possible principle of action, He adopted, and in this was a perfect example to us. All that the world needs for its renovation is the universal adoption by men of this principle.

I observe once more, and finally, that the man Christ Jesus so adhered to the principle of action He adopted as to give the highest example of heroism the world has ever known. For what is heroism? It is a firm, unfaltering adherence to the highest principle of action, self-sustained and under conditions of difficulty and hardship. Let the idea be analyzed and purified, and it will be found to be this. Think, then, how solitary and unsustained Christ was in the Garden, before the Sanhedrim, before Pilate and Herod, as He bore his cross, as He hung on that cross, as even God forsook Him, and yet He held on unfalteringly till He could utter the triumphant cry, "It is finished!" and expired. O, thou Sun of Righteousness, how didst Thou wade in darkness and in blood, that Thou mightest break forth and flood the world with thy light! Here was heroic, steadfast love, going alone into the darkness, and meeting without flinching a death of agony and of infamy. It was love that demanded it. If it had not been, the suffering would have been wantonness and folly. But not one pang could have been spared. Here, then, is a perfect example — not in its form, but in its principle — for all Christians, for ministers, for missionaries of the cross.

If, then, we look at the Scriptural idea of man as seen in the man Christ Jesus, and in those who are in Him, we find in it something vastly higher than was to be found in Adam, perfect though he was, and in the image of God. We find man, subject indeed to death, but triumphing over it and entering beyond it upon a condition of security and blessedness as much superior to that of Adam as the city of God, the New Jerusalem, is superior to the Garden of Eden. "And I saw a new heaven and a new earth." "And He that sat upon the throne said, 'Behold I make all things new.'" "He that overcometh shall inherit all things, and I will be his God and he shall be my son."

APPENDIX.

NOTE A.

THAT Democritus, Epicurus, and Lucretius had the idea of a chaos is certain, but it is equally certain that it did not originate with them. In addition to the argument in the text from the impossibility that such an idea should have been suggested by an orderly cosmos, I cite the following from the seventh chapter of Rawlinson's Ancient Monarchies: —

"The Babylonian legend embodies a primeval tradition, *common to all mankind*, of which an inspired author has given us the true groundwork in the first and second chapters of Genesis. What is especially remarkable is the fidelity, comparatively speaking, with which the Babylonian legend reports the facts. While the whole tone and spirit of the two accounts, and even the point of view from which they are taken, differ, the general outline of the narrative in each is nearly the same. In both we have the earth at first 'without form and void,' and 'darkness upon the face of the deep.' In both the first step taken towards creation is the separation of the mixed mass, and the formation of the heavens and the earth as the consequence of such separation. In both we have light mentioned before the creation of the sun and moon; in both we have the existence of animals before man; and in both we have a divine element infused into man at his birth and his formation 'from the dust of the ground.' The only points in which the narratives can be said to be at variance are points of order." He adds in a note that "the Chaldee narrative is extravagant and grotesque," while "the Mosaical is without unnecessary marvels, and its tone is sublime and solemn."

The connection between the tradition and the Hebrew Scriptures we have no means of tracing, but it is reasonable to suppose that it originated from them.

NOTE B.

In the discussions respecting development two parties seem to have been in a measure at cross purposes. Those who contend that development is consistent with theism regard it as simply a process, apart from its cause. It is for them the process by which an intelligent, all-superintending, personal God has brought the present cosmos out of chaos, working all things after the council of his own will. A person believing thus would not be called a developmentist or evolutionist. He believes the fact of development; he believes in it as a method by which God works, but he is not an evolutionist.

An evolutionist, on the other hand, is one in whose mind evolution or development is not simply a process apart from its cause, but its cause, as an inherent, unconscious, impersonal force working upward, enters in as a part of the conception of evolution, and it is that which makes him an evolutionist.

As between two parties thus situated the ground of dispute, and the only one involving anything of interest, is a question of causation, and not of development. As a process development must have a cause, and the question is whether the present order of things came to be through the agency of an intelligent, personal God wholly separate from the material with which he works and above it, or, of an unconscious impersonal force.

But besides the above there are those who do not think the present cosmos can be accounted for by any process that can be called development unless that word is used so loosely as to identify it with causation, and growth, and even with change of any kind, thus precluding its use in any profitable discussion. They regard development as a process of unfolding, expansion, enlargement. They think that anything that begins to be must be caused, and must *be*, before it can be developed. So far from agreeing with the definition that "development is organized causation," or causation at all, they think that disintegration is, or requires, organized causation quite as much. Agreeing with the Scriptures and with science that the present state of things has been reached by successive changes, they do not believe that science, any more than the Scriptures, justifies a belief in that continuity which is involved in development, but rather that the process has been one by successive preparatory steps, as in a building, and that " He that *built* all things is God."

NOTE C.

Before experience all possible events and forms of being are alike probable. Hence the boundless credulity of children. We now feel no surprise at a flash of lightning, or at the sudden formation of a cloud. Just as probable beforehand was the sudden formation of a man, and just as little should we have been surprised, if that had been the accustomed order. After experience belief is modified by the uniformities to which we are accustomed, and sometimes so strongly that they become to us the limit of possibility. But scientists make a mistake in supposing that, in a universe like this, any uniformity cognizable by man can be the limit of possibility.

When an East Indian prince was visited by an early navigator he received without question the story of Jonah and the whale with others equally marvellous, but dismissed the narrator at once when he told him that in his country water sometimes became so hard that oxen walked upon it, saying he would have nothing more to do with such a liar.

NOTE D.

To the popular definition and common conception of consciousness as "the recognition by the thinking subject of its own acts and affections," there is no objection, provided we do not at the same time make it, as thus defined, infallible, and the basis of an infallible method of philosophy. As thus defined, consciousness does sometimes give us certain knowledge, and so do the senses; but we are liable to misapprehension and delusion through both. My wish has been to find a form of consciousness with such limitations that it must always be present in connection with every other operation of the mind; that can never deceive us; and that, as not subject to the will, is not a special faculty. It is such a consciousness alone that can give us a sure basis on which to stand, and so a reliable starting-point.

As indicating the inadequacy of consciousness as above defined to give the subject of it reliable information, I quote the admirable analysis of the character of Arabi Pacha, as given by Dr. Henry M. Field in his recent work "On the Desert":—

"He seems to be compounded in about equal parts of three elements, which are the master-passions of his nature: hatred of foreigners, religious fanaticism, and personal ambition. These different impulses are so mixed up in him that probably he does not know one from another. He does not stop to analyze his motives (the Arab intellect is not given to such fine distinctions), and so he might well think he was acting from one when he was really acting from another. When he was seeking his own ambition, he believed he was seeking the good of his country, and even doing God service."

www.ingramcontent.com/pod-product-compliance
Lightning Source LLC
Chambersburg PA
CBHW030347170426
43202CB00010B/1284